Charlotte Hadfield is the head of 3PB (3 Paper Buildings) Barristers Education Group. She is a specialist in all areas of law related to education, including health, social care and employment law, and has a particular interest in exclusion and discrimination. She is listed in the Legal 500 and Chambers & Partners as a leading junior in education law. Charlotte's first introduction to education law was as a clerk for independent appeal (now review) panels. She represents excluded pupils, their parents, governing boards, and local authorities before independent review panels, in the First-tier Tribunal, and the County Court in claims for discrimination and breach of contract, and in the Administrative Court in judicial review proceedings. Charlotte has also appeared in education-related appeals before the Upper Tribunal and the Court of Appeal. Her clients appreciate her approachability, pragmatism, and user-friendly advice in conference, and her knowledge, experience, and attention to detail in hearings. Charlotte has delivered training on all aspects of education law to a variety of audiences, including parents, schools, local authorities, expert witnesses, and lawyers.

Alice de Coverley is a specialist education, equality, and public law barrister with 3PB (3 Paper Buildings) Barristers. She regularly acts on behalf of children and young people, vulnerable adults, parents and carers, schools, local authorities, charities and NGOs, government departments including Ofsted, students, and universities.

Alice has been challenging unlawful exclusion practices since she was at law school, when she was the Chief Director of the award-winning pro bono unit, the "School Exclusion Project". In 2012 the School Exclusion Project won the 'Bar Pro Bono Award'. In 2014, the School Exclusion Project was runner-up in the Attorney General LawWorks Pro Bono Awards for 'Best Contribution by a Team of Students'. Alice has also helped to create several BBC Radio 4 programmes about school exclusions. She is also ranked in both the Legal 500 and Chambers & Partners. Alice won the Legal 500 ESG 2024 "*Disability/ Neurodiversity: Bar Champion of the Year*" award. Alice was The Times' Lawyer of the Week in July 2023. She is also a Trustee of Neurodiversity in Law, a charity which aims to destigmatise and promote neurodivergence within the legal profession.

A Practical Guide to the Law in Relation to School Exclusions

Second Edition

A Practical Guide to the Law in Relation to School Exclusions

Second Edition

Charlotte Hadfield,
Barrister, Inner Temple

Alice de Coverley,
Barrister, Gray's Inn

Law Brief Publishing

Published 2024 by Law Brief Publishing, an imprint of Law Brief Publishing Ltd
30 The Parks
Minehead
Somerset
TA24 8BT

www.lawbriefpublishing.com

Paperback: 978-1-916698-62-8

To Lucy, Redmond, Caspian and Antigone

and in loving memory

of Ros and Chris Hadfield

FOREWORD

As a mother and sibling of a child with autism and complex learning needs respectively, and with 36 years collective experience working within the field of autism for Hillingdon Autistic Care and Support (HACS), a registered charity in Hillingdon, we were honoured to be approached to write the foreword for this publication.

All too often, parents find themselves in complete turmoil when the possibility of a school exclusion arrives on their doorstep. The process can be upsetting and often can be deemed 'unlawful'. A true example of this was a call we received on our telephone helpline from a parent, distressed that her son's school had contacted her to say that she needed to collect him from school each day for the lunchtime period as the school 'could not manage her son in the dining room due to his disruptive behaviour'. The parent was very distressed as this would have implications for her job, and she was unaware that this type of exclusion was unlawful. Describing her feelings the parent said, "*I am totally at my wit's end and don't know where to turn to*". Whilst we were able to give the correct advice to the parent, it would have been advantageous to signpost this parent to a publication like this book which has been written with parents, caregivers, educators and advice and guidance workers in mind. This book is an easy read whilst outlining all you need to know in relation to exclusions and ensuring schools have followed the process in a lawful manner.

All praise to the authors, for this easy-to-read publication which I would strongly advise any parent to purchase for their SEN Toolkit!

Antoinette Mullally, Chief Executive and
Lead Safeguarding Officer
Stephanie Mullally, Operations Director
Hillingdon Autistic Care and Support

CONTENTS

- Direct discrimination
    - Less favourable treatment/comparators
    - Because of a protected characteristic
    - Associative and perceptive discrimination
- Indirect discrimination
- Harassment
    - Summary
    - Harassment provisions only apply to disability, race and sex
    - Harassment related to a relevant protected characteristic
    - Sexual harassment
    - Less favourable treatment of a pupil because they submit to or reject sexual harassment or harassment related to sex
    - Purpose or effect of conduct must be to create the requisite environment
- Victimisation
    - Detriment
    - Protected act
- Discrimination arising from disability
    - Unfavourable treatment
    - Arising from the pupil's disability
    - Justification defence
    - Knowledge defence

INTRODUCTION

"It is incidental to the authority of a headmaster to expel from the school over which he presides any scholar or student whose conduct is such that he cannot any longer be permitted to remain without danger to the school. This is not a power to be exercised arbitrarily—it may be questioned; and although, no doubt, a large discretion must be allowed, it must not be exercised wantonly or capriciously."

Fitzgerald v Northcote (1865) 4 F&F 856

In 1865, David Fitzgerald, a 17-year-old schoolboy, and his father, a reputable Irish Judge, brought a claim for damages against Rev. S. Northcote, and Rev. W. Stone, the headmasters of a school, for assault and false imprisonment, on the occasion of David's permanent exclusion.

David was a pupil at a school which had a cohort of both lay students and clerical students. It was alleged that David, a lay student, had set up a secret society against the clerical students – the "*Anti-Bunker Confederacy*" – and had "*entered into, and engaged in, mischievous and invidious inquiries as to the birth and parentage of* [the clerical students], *such as might lead to bad and injurious consequences, and might endanger the peace and harmony of the school*". Consequently, David was permanently excluded for his "*mischievous disposition*", after being locked in his room. His pocketbook, allegedly containing all his notes on these clerical pupils, was forced from him.

In a letter explaining the exclusion decision to David's father, Rev. Northcote wrote:

"Anything more ungentlemanly in itself, or more mischievous in its public consequences I have rarely, I may say never, met with since my connexion with the College. Even if it had been his first offence, I should have felt it my duty to mark my sense of such conduct by some very serious penalty; but, after all his antecedents of this half-year, I

> *had no alternative but to dismiss him immediately. I need not say how much it has cost me to have recourse to so extreme a measure with a boy of his promise, and after so many years' residence among us."*

In those days, claims for damages were heard by juries. The jury was asked to consider the following questions:

> "1. *Was the plaintiff a pupil under the care and governance of the defendants, and subject to the rules and discipline of the school? If not, of course he could not be expelled for breach of that discipline. 2. Was a secret society formed or originated among the students injurious to a certain class of them? 3. Was the plaintiff a member and promoter of that society? 4. Had the defendants' reasonable grounds to believe, that such a society existed, and that the plaintiff was a member of it? 5. Was it necessary, with a view to maintain the good order and discipline of the school, that the defendants should be acquainted with the constitution of the society, and that, with that view, they should demand and take the book? 6. If so, did they use more violence than necessary? 7. Were the circumstances such as to justify the defendants in the reasonable exercise of their authority in expelling the plaintiff? 8. If so, was it necessary, for the purpose of preserving the discipline of the school, to prevent him from communicating with the other students? 9. If so, was it necessary for that purpose to lock him in his room? 10. If it was not so necessary, had the defendants' reasonable grounds for believing that the course pursued was necessary to preserve the' maintenance of discipline?"*

The jury found in favour of David and awarded him damages of £5 (approximately £632 in today's money).

It is evident from this Victorian case, even prior to the introduction of any statutory framework for exclusions through subsequent Education Acts, that the principle of reasonableness has been central to exclusion decisions for some time. Exclusion was well within the headmasters' discretion, but evidently "*not a power to be exercised arbitrarily*" and only when there was *"reasonable cause".* [1] Exclusion was, and remains, something capable of being scrutinised.

Nowadays, exclusion of pupils from a maintained school, academy, or pupil referral unit, for a fixed period or permanently, is permitted under the Education Act 2002. Under s 52, several sets of regulations have been issued, governing how and when such decisions are to be made.[2] These regulations must be observed by head teachers, governing bodies, local authorities and Independent Review Panels as appropriate. These parties must also have regard to statutory government guidance issued under s 52.[3]

---

1 Such discretion not being absolute. See *Hutt v Governors of Haileybury College* (1888) 4 TLR 623

2 The current provisions are, in England, the School Discipline (Pupil Exclusions and Reviews) (England) (Amendment and Transitional Provision) Regulations 2023, the School Discipline (Pupil Exclusions and Reviews) (England) Regulations 2012 and the Education (Provision of Full-Time Education for Excluded Pupils) (England) Regulations 2007, as amended by the Education (Provision of Full-Time Education for Excluded Pupils) (England) (Amendment) Regulations 2014 (amending the Education (Provision of Full-Time Education for Excluded Pupils) (England) Regulations 2007). In Wales the current provisions are The Education (Pupil Exclusions and Appeals) (Pupil Referral Units) (Wales) (Amendment) Regulations 2024, the Education (Pupil Exclusions and Appeals) (Maintained Schools) (Wales) Regulations 2003, and the Education (Pupil Exclusions and Appeals) (Pupil Referral Units) (Wales) Regulations 2003, as amended by the Education (Pupil Exclusions and Appeals) (Wales) (Miscellaneous Amendments) Regulations 2004. See also the Education (Reintegration Interview) (Wales) Regulations 2010.

3 See Education Act 2002, section 52(4)(b). The relevant statutory guidance in England is the DfE publication *Suspension and Permanent Exclusion from maintained schools, academies and pupil referral units in England, including pupil movement: Guidance for maintained schools, academies, and pupil referral units in England* the DfE's statutory guidance

In England, a decision to exclude a pupil permanently from a maintained school, academy or pupil referral unit should only be taken where there has been a serious breach, or persistent breaches, of the school's behaviour policy; *and* where allowing the pupil to remain in school would seriously harm the education or welfare of the pupil or others in the school. Pupils cannot lawfully be excluded if they have not breached the school's behaviour policy. The decision to exclude a pupil must be lawful, reasonable, procedurally fair, and proportionate.

In Wales, a decision to exclude a learner should be taken only in response to serious breaches of the school's behaviour policy *and* where allowing the learner to remain in school would seriously harm the education or welfare of the learner or others in the school. This means that first or one-off offences should only exceptionally lead to permanent exclusion in Wales.

Independent schools, unlike maintained schools and academies, do not have to follow the statutory school exclusion guidance. Decisions relating to exclusions are largely subject to contract law principles. The preliminary mechanism for formal challenge is generally the school's complaints procedure; any subsequent court remedy would most likely be via a claim in contract or under the Equality Act 2010.

Any decision of a maintained school, including exclusion, must be made in line with the principles of administrative law, i.e. that it is: lawful (that is, in accordance with the law relating specifically to exclusion, and also with a school's wider legal duties under, for example, the Human Rights Act and the Equality Act); rational; reasonable; procedurally fair; and proportionate.

In other jurisdictions, decisions to permanently exclude pupils from schools similarly require additional oversight and approval by school

on school exclusions, most recently updated in August 2024. For Wales, see *Exclusion from schools and pupil referral units*, updated in April 2024.

boards (such as in various US and Canadian states). In New Zealand, the exclusion decision *must* be taken by the school's board – it cannot be carried out directly by the principal. In mainland China, exclusions of pupils of compulsory education schools are completely prohibited.[4]

Focus on school exclusions has intensified in recent years, following an increased emphasis on behaviour and attitudes in schools and rising levels of permanent and fixed-period exclusions.[5] Exclusion from school can be a life-changing event for a pupil with profoundly negative consequences for their future. Pupils who have been excluded are unlikely to reach the same levels of academic achievement as their peers, making it more difficult for them to progress to further study and work. Exclusion negatively impacts upon children's mental health, reinforcing their sense of rejection and negative self-image. [6] It can also increase their vulnerability to criminal exploitation.[7]

---

4 Under Article 27 of the Compulsory Education Act 2006: *"For a student who violates the school management rules, the school shall criticize and educate him/her, but shall not expel him/her from school."*

5 Gill, Quilter-Pinner and Swift, 'Making the Difference: Breaking the Link between School Exclusion and Social Exclusion' Institute for Public Policy Research (2017) p. 21, available at https://www.ippr.org/files/2017-10/making-the-difference-report-october-2017.pdf

6 Ford at al., 'The Relationship between Exclusion from School and Mental Health: A Secondary Analysis of the British Child and Adolescent Mental Health Surveys 2004 and 2007' Psychological Medicine (25 August 2017) available at https://ore.exeter.ac.uk/repository/handle/10871/28337

7 'School Exclusions "Fuelling Gang Violence"' BBC News (30 October 2018) available at https://www.bbc.com/news/uk-46027265; House of Commons Home Affairs Committee, 'Serious Youth Violence: Sixteenth Report of Session 2017-19' (2019) paras 163-171, available at https://publications.parliament.uk/pa/cm201719/cmselect/cmhaff/1016/1016.pdf; Timpson p. 8.

In May 2019, Edward Timpson published his landmark school exclusions review, commissioned by the Secretary of State for Education.[8] The Timpson review explored the use of exclusion by head teachers in practice, children's personal experiences of exclusion, and why some children are more likely to be excluded than others. These include those who have been identified by their local authority as children in need, those with special educational needs[9] ("SEN"), and children who have been supported by social care, who are eligible for free school meals, or are from particular ethnic groups. The findings from this report highlighted the ways in which exclusion can disproportionately affect those from particular social groups:

> *"The analysis produced for this review shows that 78% of permanent exclusions issued were to pupils who either had SEN, were classified as in need or were eligible for free school meals. 11% of permanent exclusions were to pupils who had all three characteristics."*

Timpson made various recommendations for improvements to the school exclusion system, including that:

> *"DfE should update statutory guidance on exclusion to provide more clarity on the use of exclusion. DfE should also ensure all relevant, overlapping guidance (including behaviour management, exclusion, mental health and behaviour, guidance on the role of the designated teacher for looked after and previously looked after children and the SEND Code of Practice) is clear, accessible and consistent in its messages to help schools manage additional needs, create positive behaviour cultures, make reasonable adjustments under the Equality Act 2010 and use exclusion only as a last resort, when nothing else will do. Guidance should also include information on robust and well-*

8 http://data.parliament.uk/DepositedPapers/Files/DEP2019-0527/Timpson_Review_of_School_Exclusion_May_2019.pdf

9 Children Act 1989, section 17

> *evidenced strategies that will support schools embedding this in practice."*

When publishing the first edition of this book in 2020, the DfE was yet to launch a consultation or update its statutory school exclusion guidance as a consequence of the Timpson review.

The Government, however, got to work in 2022 and 2023, updating the statutory school exclusions guidance twice, and substantially, following public consultation. This book sets out all changes in law and guidance as of 1st October 2024.

The new suspensions and permanent exclusions guidance clarified various aspects of law and procedure, including the role of the SEN expert, virtual school heads, and social workers at hearings. The new guidance also makes clearer how remote hearings can be used (though not as standard practice) as well as tidied up how managed moves, off-site direction, and cancellations of exclusions should operate.

The new guidance also refers throughout to "suspensions" as opposed to the statutory language of fixed-term exclusions. Suspension is still defined as an exclusion for a fixed period. "No exclusion" policies are prohibited. Part-time timetables are discouraged as a measure to manage pupil behaviour. More detail is included regarding a school's important welfare and safeguarding duties and how to work with other agencies, such as the police and social care, where appropriate. Preventative measures to exclusion are far more strongly emphasised in the new guidance. Pupil's views are central. Local authorities must be notified of all suspensions and exclusions, including those where the total has not exceeded five school days in the current term. Sources of free legal advice have been expanded. Governors are required to scrutinise and evaluate what the school's data is telling them about pupil movement and the protected characteristics of those who are being suspended or excluded, or sent for off-site direction. The guidance links better to the Children and Families Act 2014 and the Equality Act 2010 (not enough, in our view, leading to a significant flurry of appellate case law the authors have been involved in to clarify the position).

Much additional work is being done to analyse the factors that give rise to disproportionate rates of exclusion for children with different protected characteristics. In November 2019, JUSTICE launched its working party report, *'Challenging School Exclusions'* which called for significant overhaul of the current system.[10] This included suggestions for better training for schools on excluding pupils, an entirely new Independent Reviewer of individual exclusion decisions, and the possibility of appealing to a judge-led tribunal.

There has also been greater recognition of the effect of increasingly challenging working conditions upon teachers, some of whom can face unacceptable levels of violence from their students.[11]

There has also been greater awareness and scrutiny of 'off-rolling' practices by schools. This followed high-profile legal proceedings in 2017 involving St Olave's, a grammar school in Orpington, London. This school had a policy that restricted access to the upper sixth form (Year 13) to those who achieved top grades. The result was that a number of students were pushed out at the end of Year 12, and left struggling to find places elsewhere to finish their two-year A Level course. Following allegations that this practice amounted to unlawful exclusion,[12] the school reversed the policy.

---

10 Joanna Williams, "It Just Grinds You Down", 17th December 2018, Policy Exchange (available at https://justice.org.uk/wp-content/uploads/2019/11/Challenging-Report.pdf)

11 Ibid.

12 https://www.theguardian.com/education/2017/aug/29/grammar-school-unlawfully-threw-out-students-who-failed-to-get-top-grades

Ofsted inspectors now look for evidence of off-rolling as part of their inspection. Ofsted's working definition of off-rolling is currently:

> *"the practice of removing a pupil from the school roll without using a permanent exclusion, when the removal is primarily in the best interests of the school, rather than the best interests of the pupil. This includes pressuring a parent to remove their child from the school roll."*[13]

The rate of suspensions and permanent exclusions, nonetheless, continue to increase. This is despite the shift in the statutory guidance towards considering alternatives to exclusion.

Statistics released by the Department for Education in July 2024 showed a record-high number of exclusions issued by schools. There were 9,376 permanent exclusions in 2022/2023, up from 6,495 in 2021/2022, alongside 786,961 suspensions in 2022/2023, up from 578,280 in 2021/2022. This is the equivalent of 11 permanent exclusions for every 10,000 pupils, and 933 suspensions for every 10,000 pupils. Persistent disruptive behaviour accounted for 48% of all reasons recorded for suspension and for 39% of reasons recorded for permanent exclusions.

As to the reasons recorded for exclusions, The Evening Standard launched a campaign in May 2024 to create a new data category for excluding pupils that encompassed sexist abuse, sexual harassment and violence against girls, expanding the existing 16 categories under which a head teacher can file an exclusion decision. Since 2021, the Government has added five further reasons for exclusion to the list that schools need to file decisions under — among them "inappropriate use of social media" and "transgression of protective measures to protect public health", a response to Covid — but, despite increased calls, a category for sexual abuse or harassment has not yet had a look in.

---

13 https://educationinspection.blog.gov.uk/2019/05/10/what-is-off-rolling-and-how-does-ofsted-look-at-it-on-inspection/

Exclusions and Covid-19

Of particular concern to us is the educational disruption that was caused by the Covid-19 pandemic, both generally and specifically in relation to school exclusions. This produced potential new and heightened risks for pupils, underpinned by the increased rate of exclusions above. According to research from the University of Oxford (released on 22 June 2020),[14] Ian Thompson, Associate Professor of Education at Oxford:

> *"The social and emotional disruption caused by the pandemic and the subsequent school closures is highly likely to have increased or exacerbated student anxiety and other mental health issues. There is also a concern with school connectedness for vulnerable students, whose patterns of school attendance have been disrupted. These concerns raise issues around transitions back to school settings"*

Professor Harry Daniels added, *'All children will have experienced some adverse effects from the Covid-19 pandemic, but for some these will be traumatic and long-lasting and this may impact negatively on whether and how they return to school, and the likelihood of formal, informal and self-exclusion.'*

Between 1 June 2020 and 24 September 2020, new arrangements were put in place for the school exclusion process, due to Covid-19. The relevant regulations for this period were the School Discipline (England) (Coronavirus) (Pupil Exclusions and Reviews) (Amendment) Regulations 2020.

The DfE's statutory guidance remained in place during the pandemic, save for changes to the timescales for the meeting of governing boards, for applications for review, and to arrange meetings of Independent Review Panels. Remote access hearings were also being made available. This is because governing boards and independent review panels were

14 http://www.ox.ac.uk/news/2020-06-22-risks-school-exclusions-england-may-be-higher-after-covid-19

not permitted to conduct paper-based hearings. Exclusion decisions made during this period had still to be lawful, fair, proportionate, and non-discriminatory. Readers consulting this book and considering exclusion decisions during the Covid-19 pandemic are advised to check the Government's website for all guidance it produced during the 2020-2022 period of the pandemic.[15]

What this book is about

In the second edition of this book, we offer a practical legal guide to the current school exclusion regime in England as it stands on 1st October 2024, four years since our first edition. We aim to make this book as helpful as possible to parents, young people, school staff, and specialist representatives. We hope that it may be a useful resource for those who appear on behalf of children and young people, or schools, or governing bodies, before Independent Review Panels and the First-tier Tribunal.

In **Chapter 1**, we look at school discipline, exclusion being the most serious disciplinary sanction a school can impose. This chapter summarises the rules and regulations relating to behaviour policies (which all schools must have in place); the power to sanction pupils for bad behaviour and the range of sanctions (short of permanent exclusion) generally available to schools, including detentions, seclusion/isolation and fixed-period exclusions; the powers to screen, search and confiscate in schools; misconduct outside of school; the power to use reasonable force; social media, internet and "cyberbullying"; and the power to direct pupils off-site to improve behaviour.

Chapters 2 and 3 focus on permanent exclusion in maintained schools and academies. In **Chapter 2** we focus upon the first instance decision to exclude taken by the head teacher, including the importance of early

15 https://www.gov.uk/government/publications/school-exclusion/changes-to-the-school-exclusion-process-during-the-coronavirus-outbreak

intervention; investigation of the circumstances giving rise to the decision whether or not to permanently exclude; when permanent exclusion is lawful; alternatives to permanent exclusion, such as managed moves and Alternative Provision; and administrative concerns such as the rules around recording a permanent exclusion and the local authority's duties following exclusion. We also provide a (non-exhaustive) list of factors that may potentially be relevant to a decision to exclude.

In **Chapter 3**, staying with permanent exclusion in maintained schools and academies, we examine the statutory scheme for review of decisions to exclude. We look at the governing board's duty to review a permanent exclusion and the remit of the Independent Review Panel. We look at the role of the SEN expert, the social worker, and the pupil voice. Where the pupil facing exclusion has or may have a disability, this chapter should be read in conjunction with Chapter 6.

Chapter 4 examines the role of judicial review in school exclusions. The majority of challenges to exclusion decisions are resolved via the Independent Review Panel process. However, judicial review remains a valuable if somewhat limited means of challenging unlawful decisions by the Independent Review Panel, and reconsiderations by governing boards where the Independent Review Panel has so ordered, in respect of which there is no statutory right of review. Judicial review's main relevance is to exclusions in maintained schools and academies; it has little if any application in the independent sector (as to which see Chapter 5). In this chapter, we provide a broad summary of principles and procedure in relation to judicial review claims, and review some of the public law decisions that have been made in the area of school exclusion.

Chapter 5 provides a guide to permanent exclusion decisions in independent schools. Independent schools, unlike maintained schools and academies, do not have to follow the statutory school exclusion guidance. Parents can invoke the complaints procedure as a means of triggering a review of an exclusion by the school's governing board, but their decisions are not subject to review by the Independent Review Panel. Public law principles have very little application in what is essentially a private law relationship between parents and independent schools, regulated largely by the terms of the contract between them, and so the legality of any exclusion from an independent school is likely to turn upon principles of commercial contract law. However, independent schools are subject to the Equality Act 2010, just as maintained schools and academies are, and so Chapter 6 (discrimination) will be of relevance to parents and pupils of independent schools who believe that they or their child has been the subject of a discriminatory exclusion.

Chapter 6 of this book provides an overview of the Equality Act 2010, which applies to all schools including independent schools. In this chapter, we summarise some key concepts in the Equality Act, including protected characteristics, prohibited conduct, some common defences, and the liability of responsible bodies of schools. We offer an overview of bringing claims for discrimination in the First-tier Tribunal and the County Court; the burden and standard of proof in Equality Act claims; the remedies available in each jurisdiction; and the Public Sector Equality Duty. We also set out relevant discrimination case law up to 2024, given the recent spate of helpful Upper Tribunal decisions relevant to disability discrimination.

In the **Appendix**, we have listed some information about support and advocacy groups for excluded children and their parents.

We would like to thank Rose and Jos, and our barrister and clerking colleagues in the Education Group at 3PB.

Charlotte Hadfield
Alice de Coverley
October 2024

CHAPTER ONE

SCHOOL DISCIPLINE

Introduction and Overview

Fixed-period and permanent exclusions are sanctions for pupil misconduct. They are at the top end of a range of disciplinary sanctions which may be imposed upon pupils who break school rules. The purpose of school discipline is to promote good pupil behaviour, rewarding good conduct and penalising bad, whether occurring in school or (in some circumstances) outside.

Discipline prepares pupils for adulthood and employment. However, the exercise of discipline must be lawful. The permanent exclusion of a pupil is a substantial and serious step and should not be taken lightly. Exclusion causes substantial distress to pupils, as discussed in the Introduction, whether they have committed a very serious one-off offence, or have been persistently disruptive for some time. It can have a significant effect on their future and life chances. Parents and carers of pupils will usually also experience great distress – even devastation – at the prospect of their child's permanent exclusion from school. Many parents' instinctive reaction to an exclusion will be to ask why some lesser sanction was not considered, or was not considered sufficient; or why some potential alternative intervention – a referral to CAMHS, an assessment for learning difficulties, a managed move – was not put in place instead.

These are all questions that lead to careful examination of the school's behaviour policy and the extent to which the school abided by it or departed from it. Any material procedural flaw, failure to observe natural justice or illegality in the decision-making process that might undermine the validity of the decision to exclude is potentially helpful to a parent seeking to challenge an exclusion. (For a summary of the paths of review available, see Chapter 3 in relation to maintained schools and academies;

Chapter 5 in relation to independent schools; and Chapter 6 in relation to discrimination.)

The behaviour policy is also of critical importance in discrimination claims. If an exclusion is challenged as discriminatory (whether that is before the Independent Review Panel in conjunction with other shortcomings, or by way of a claim in the First-tier Tribunal or the County Court), all parties should expect the court or tribunal to look with particular care at the behaviour policy: whether the policy is compliant with the law, including the Equality Act 2010; whether the school followed its policy in making the decision that it did; whether reasonable adjustments should have been made to any part of the policy. If the school appears to have materially departed from its behaviour policy in a way that caused disadvantage to the pupil, or there are other legal errors in the decision to exclude, this may give rise to an inference that the exclusion was discriminatory as well as unlawful. (See Chapter 6 in relation to the Equality Act.)

In our view, an understanding of the law relating to discipline is important both for head teachers and governors making decisions in relation to exclusions, and for parents seeking to challenge a decision to exclude. Accordingly, this book starts by summarising powers and duties of schools in relation to discipline and behaviour, and considering a number of areas of discipline which may be relevant to a decision to exclude.

School's duty to put in place and review a behaviour policy

The governing body of a maintained school must ensure that policies designed to promote good pupil behaviour and discipline are pursued at the school, and that it is periodically reviewed.[16] The head teacher has

16 Education and Inspections Act 2006, section 89(6)

responsibility for pupil behaviour and discipline[17] . The behaviour policy must be published on the school's website. [18] Governing bodies of maintained schools must make arrangements to ensure that their functions are carried out with a view to safeguarding and promoting the welfare of children.[19]

Similar (though not identical) rules apply to independent schools and academies. They must have in place a written behaviour policy that sets out, amongst other matters, the sanctions that will be used if a pupil misbehaves. The policy must be implemented effectively, and the school must keep a record of the sanctions given to pupils for serious misbehaviour.[20] There is also a requirement to produce and implement an anti-bullying policy. Particulars of the policy on misbehaviour and exclusions must be made available to parents of pupils and prospective pupils, as well as to the Chief Inspector, the Secretary of State for Education and an independent inspectorate upon request. [21] Most independent schools and academies will achieve this by publishing the policy on the Internet, although there is no specific requirement to do so. The proprietors of academies and independent schools must make arrangements to safeguard and promote the welfare of pupils at the school. Such arrangements must have regard to guidance issued by the DfE. [22]

---

17 Education and Inspections Act 2006, section 89(1)

18 School Information (England) Regulations 2008 (as amended by the School Information (England) (Amendment) Regulations 2012), schedule 4, paragraph 8.

19 Education Act 2002 section 175(2)

20 Education (Independent School Standards) Regulations 2014, Schedule Part 3, paragraph 9

21 Education (Independent School Standards) Regulations 2014, Schedule Part 6, paragraphs 31(1)(b) and 31(3)(a))

22 Education (Independent School Standards) Regulations 2014, Schedule

The head teacher must set out measures in the behaviour policy which aim to promote good behaviour, self-discipline and respect; prevent bullying; ensure that pupils complete assigned work; and regulate the conduct of pupils.[23] It is for the head teacher to determine the standard of behaviour expected of pupils; the school rules; and the penalties for breaking the rules.

The governing body of a school must make, and periodically review, a written statement of general principles (in relation to behaviour), and the head teacher must have regard to this in deciding what measures to include in the policy.[24] The head teacher must also have regard to any guidance or notification that the governing body has given as to any particular measures that should be included in the policy.[25]

Content of the behaviour policy

The purpose of the behaviour policy is to ensure that pupils and parents have a clear understanding of the standards of behaviour expected within the school, what is and is not permitted in school by way of conduct, what sanctions might be applied and in what circumstances. It is also the means by which teachers and staff at the school understand the measures that are available to them to promote good behaviour and discourage or penalise bad behaviour, when certain sanctions can be used and by whom. Different schools may prioritise different disciplinary issues, and disciplinary priorities may change over time. It is essential that the behaviour policy clearly reflects the current position.

A behaviour policy is likely to provide for sanctions that escalate if the original offence is aggravated: for example, minor misconduct such as

---

Part 3, paragraph 7

23 Education and Inspections Act 2006 section 89(1)

24 Education and Inspections Act 2006, section 88(2)(a)

25 Education and Inspections Act 2006, section 88(2)(b)

talking when the teacher has asked for silence or being caught eating in class, may merit a verbal reprimand. If the pupil refuses to stop the conduct in question, or repeats it, they may end up with a detention. The way in which sanctions may escalate and in what circumstances should be set out clearly in the behaviour policy. In particular, it will explain the decision-making process and the relevant factors around a decision to temporarily exclude and to permanently exclude.

However, the behaviour policy should go further than a description of offences and sanctions. As already noted, if an exclusion is challenged, the school's behaviour policy will be examined in detail. A behaviour policy should address the school's position in relation to the following (and/or clearly refer to other relevant policies if they exist):

- The circumstances in which reasonable force may be used by staff with respect to pupils
- A definition of persistent disruptive behaviour and the interventions that will be considered/obtained. The policy should set out when assistance from other agencies will be sought, and which agencies might be approached. These might include the local authority responsible for the child, the Educational Psychology service, CAMHS, Speech & Language Therapy, Occupational Therapy, specialist teachers (ASD, dyslexia, visual impairments, hearing impairments etc.)
- Circumstances in which managed moves may be considered as an alternative to permanent exclusion (as to managed moves and other alternatives to exclusion, see Chapter 2)
- The use of social media, the internet and IT facilities
- The circumstances in which pupils may be disciplined for behaviour taking place off school premises

- The use of screening, searches and confiscation
- Any "zero-tolerance" policies (most commonly this relates to supply and use of alcohol/illegal drugs, especially on school premises; bullying and harassment; and discrimination)
- A list of banned items (including but not limited to prohibited items as described below)
- The approach to be taken to reasonable adjustments of the behaviour policy for disabled pupils under the Equality Act 2010 who might (for example) find it harder to regulate their behaviour on a two-strikes rule and who would otherwise end up with a disproportionate number of formal sanctions on their record due to their disability. (As to discrimination generally, see Chapter 6.)

Early intervention: is the behaviour policy fit for purpose?

In Chapter 2 we look at the importance of early intervention in cases where there is persistent disruptive behaviour or other signs that a pupil is starting to struggle. If there is a permanent exclusion, the Independent Review Panel will be alive to any missed opportunities to identify and support a pupil who is obviously in difficulties, whether due to unidentified SEN or some other reason. This is also of considerable importance in the context of discrimination claims arising from exclusion. The DfE recommends[26] that as part of their early intervention strategy, the head teacher should have processes for identifying and supporting additional needs. This includes reviewing the behaviour policy periodically to ensure that:

---

26 Exclusion from maintained schools, academies and pupil referral units in England, DfE statutory guidance, September 2023, page 10

- the behaviour policy clearly sets out behaviour expectations and sanctions, and is compliant with the Equality Act 2010 (see Chapter 6 on discrimination);
- governors and staff, including sixth form staff, are clear about their roles and when to escalate issues or involve parents
- pupils and parents understand the behaviour policy
- sanctions are monitored to identify any inconsistency or potential discrimination (e.g. SEN, disability or ethnicity)
- systems are in place to identify pupils showing persistent poor behaviour, and any underlying causes.

The power to sanction pupils for bad behaviour

A teacher, or a paid member of staff authorised to do so by the head teacher, may impose a disciplinary penalty upon a pupil if the pupil's conduct falls below the standard which could reasonably be expected.[27]

Teachers can lawfully sanction a pupil whose behaviour falls below the standard expected provided that 3 conditions are met:[28]

- The decision in relation to sanction must be made by a paid member of school staff or a member of staff authorised by the head teacher.
- The decision (not necessarily the underlying conduct being sanctioned) must be made on the school premises, or whilst the

27 Education and Inspections Act 2006 section 90(1)

28 Education and Inspections Act 2006 section 90(3)–(5)

pupil is under the charge of the member of staff making the decision.

- The sanction must not breach any other legislation (e.g. the Equality Act 2010) and must be reasonable in all circumstances.

The following factors must be taken into account in deciding whether the imposition of the penalty is reasonable:[29]

- Whether it is proportionate in all the circumstances
- The pupil's age, any SEN or disability[30] that they may have, and any religious requirements affecting them.

In addition, the decision-maker may take into account any other special circumstances that affect the pupil.

The range of potential disciplinary sanctions

Schools are advised to have in place a range of options and rewards to reinforce and praise good behaviour, as well as sanctions for those whose behaviour falls below the required standard.[31] These should be set out and fully described in the behaviour policy, and the circumstances in which each may be used should be fully explained.

Sanctions may include:

- Verbal reprimand

---

29 Education and Inspections Act 2006 section 91(6)

30 Within the meaning of the Equality Act 2010: see Chapter 6

31 *Behaviour and discipline in schools: Advice for headteachers and school staff*, DfE departmental advice, February 2024, page 27

- Extra work/repeating work until it meets the standard required
- Written tasks as sanctions, e.g. writing lines
- Loss of privileges (e.g. removal of a prestigious responsibility, withdrawal from a school-wide treat such as non-uniform days)
- Missing break time
- School-based community service or tasks such as litter-picking, weeding school grounds, tidying, helping to clear up the dining hall or removing graffiti
- Regular reporting, e.g. early morning reporting, scheduled uniform or other behaviour checks, or being placed "on report" for behaviour monitoring
- Detention during lunchtime, after school and at weekends
- "Isolations" or "seclusions"
- Internal exclusions (a relatively new mechanism used by some schools as an alternative to a fixed-period exclusion; as yet there is neither DfE guidance in relation to internal exclusions, nor case law determining its lawfulness)
- Fixed-period exclusions
- Permanent exclusion (see Chapter 2)

There are two further measures that can be taken that might well feel like sanctions to a pupil, but may be better described as supportive measures of last resort:

- Directing a pupil off-site to improve their behaviour (discussed later in this chapter).

- Managed moves. These are sometimes used in circumstances where a pupil's behaviour is such that they cannot stay at their current school, but mitigating circumstances exist that might justify arranging a move to another school by agreement, rather than a permanent exclusion. Managed moves are discussed further in Chapter 2.

Corporal punishment

Corporal punishment is unlawful in all circumstances and in all types of schools. This includes religious schools, independent schools and boarding schools. [32] In some limited circumstances, teachers are permitted to use reasonable force to restrain pupils, which is addressed below. However, it is always unlawful, and never reasonable, to use force as a punishment.

Detentions

Paid staff authorised by the head teacher may lawfully issue detentions to pupils aged under 18, without parental consent. They may authorise all staff, including support staff, to impose detentions,[33] or certain categories of staff (e.g. heads of year or department). It is good practice to set this out in the behaviour policy so that staff, pupils and parents are clear about who can issue a detention to a pupil.

Schools must make it clear to pupils and parents that detentions (including detentions outside of school hours) are used as a sanction. The best way to do this is to set it out in the behaviour policy. Detentions can

---

32 *R (Williamson and Others) v Secretary of State for Education and Employment* [2005] UKHL 15

33 Education and Inspections Act 2006, section 91(4)

be given on any school day where the pupil does not have permission to be absent; weekends (except the weekend preceding or following the half-term break); and INSET days (non-teaching days where staff are receiving training). This includes detention outside of normal school hours, provided that:[34]

- The pupil is under 18
- The head teacher has previously determined, and has made it generally known within school and to parents of pupils, that this is a disciplinary measure that may be used
- The detention is on a permitted day of detention
- (in Wales) that the pupil's parent has been given at least 24 hours' notice in writing that the detention is due to take place.

Staff should consider whether imposing the detention is likely to put the pupil at risk; whether the pupil has known caring responsibilities meaning that the detention is unreasonable; and whether the parents should be informed of the detention (it will often be necessary to do so, but not always, although most schools will attempt to inform parents on the same day).[35]

Detentions can sometimes cause parents considerable inconvenience – travel arrangements can become complicated for parents who work in the evening or have other children to take to extracurricular activities. Schools do have to consider whether suitable travel arrangements can be made by the parent for the pupil in deciding whether to impose a detention and on what day. However, provided that suitable travel arrangements can be made it does not matter if this is inconvenient for

---

34 Education and Inspections Act 2006, section 92(2) and (3)

35 *Behaviour and discipline in schools: Advice for headteachers and school staff*, DfE departmental advice February 2024, page 23

the parent[36] (subject obviously to any Equality Act duties that the school may owe to the parent as a service user).

Staff considering issuing a detention must also have regard to any special educational need or disability that the pupil has and the school's duties to the pupil under the Equality Act 2010: see Chapter 6. Schools should make it clear in their behaviour policies that they will make reasonable adjustments to the behaviour policy where appropriate for disabled pupils (which is likely to include all pupils receiving extra help or provision due to identified learning disabilities or SEN).

Seclusion or isolation

Some schools have a policy of placing disruptive pupils in an area away from other pupils for a limited period. This is often called isolation or seclusion. Some schools have introduced "isolation booths" as a disciplinary sanction, in addition to or combined with the concept of internal exclusion. Isolation booths tend to be small spaces in which pupils sit alone, usually in silence, as a sanction for breaking school rules or for disruptive behaviour.

The DfE advises that if a school uses this method of sanction it must say so clearly in its behaviour policy, and that schools must act reasonably in all the circumstances when using such rooms. It goes on to say that any isolation that prevents a child from leaving the room of their own free will should be considered only in exceptional circumstances, and that the health, safety, and welfare of pupils must be ensured. Schools must not keep pupils in seclusion or isolation longer than is necessary, and their time must be used as constructively as possible; they must be permitted reasonable time to eat (e.g. lunch) and use the toilet.[37]

---

36 *Behaviour and discipline in schools: Advice for headteachers and school staff*, DfE departmental advice February 2024, page 21

37 *Behaviour and discipline in schools: Advice for headteachers and school staff*,

There is, as yet, no case law regarding the use of isolation as a disciplinary sanction. However, the Children's Commissioner has expressed concerns about this sanction and is conducting research into the use of such booths. In particular, there is a concern that isolation disproportionately affects children with SEN and disabilities. [38] The new Labour Government has included discipline in its review of measures used by schools to manage behaviour, with isolation booths said to be being phased out.

Fixed-period exclusions

Overview

Section 51A(1) of the Education Act 2002[39] allows head teachers of maintained schools, [40] ("PRUs") to issue fixed-period or permanent exclusions. These are the most severe sanctions available to schools. Permanent exclusion is considered in Chapter 2. Here we look at fixed-period exclusions. These are now formally known as 'suspensions' though the legislative underpinning remains the same.

A fixed-period exclusion may only be given to a pupil for disciplinary reasons. Pupils may not be excluded because they have SEN or are disabled, or because of any other protected characteristic; nor may they be excluded because of the behaviour of their parents; nor may they be excluded on the ground of their academic ability or attainment. The

---

DfE departmental advice February 2024 page 21

38 https://www.theguardian.com/education/2020/jan/17/schools-converting-toilet-blocks-into-isolation-booths

39 As amended by the Education Act 2011, section 4

40 This means a community, foundation or voluntary school, a community or foundation special school or a maintained nursery school – Education Act 2002, section 1(3), as amended by the Education and Inspections Act 2006 section 1(4).

behaviour of a pupil outside school, however, can be considered grounds for a fixed-period exclusion by the head teacher.

Is a further fixed-period exclusion an effective sanction?

The DfE advises that where a pupil has received multiple exclusions, or is approaching the legal limit of 45 school days of exclusion in an academic year, the head teacher should give consideration to whether exclusion is an effective sanction..[41] Later in this section we look at the importance of early intervention and support in circumstances where a pupil is exhibiting persistent disruptive behaviour and/or is considered to be at risk of permanent exclusion. Any forum considering the legality of an exclusion will expect to see evidence of serious attempts at early intervention for pupils exhibiting persistent disruptive behaviour or other signs that they are vulnerable to exclusion.

Duration of a fixed-term exclusion (suspension)

Since an exclusion can only be for a fixed period (i.e. a fixed number of days), or permanent, an exclusion cannot be for an indefinite period; they must be for a fixed number of days.[42] Exclusions cannot be given for an unspecified or indefinite period, for example until a meeting can be arranged. Any exclusion of a pupil, even for short periods of time, must be formally recorded. Informal or unofficial exclusions, such as sending pupils home to "cool off", are unlawful, even if the pupil's parents or carers have agreed to this approach.[43] There are strict requirements in relation to recording fixed-period exclusions, which are set out below.

---

41 Suspension and Permanent Exclusion from maintained schools, academies and pupil referral units in England, including pupil movement, DfE statutory guidance, August 2024, para 6

42 Education Act 2002, section 51A

43 Suspension and Permanent Exclusion from maintained schools, academies and pupil referral units in England, including pupil

Lisa falls out with her best friend and puts up a number of abusive posts on social media, directed by name at her friend. The head teacher orders Lisa to take down the posts. Lisa refuses to do so. The head teacher says that if she does not do this he will suspend her. Lisa refuses again and is sent home at 11am with a letter to her parents stating that Lisa "has been sent home from school for cyberbullying, and may not come back to school until she removes the abusive content that she has posted". This is an indefinite exclusion, because it has no fixed term, and is therefore unlawful.

A pupil may be excluded for one or more fixed periods, up to a total of 45 days excluded from school. This is the case whether the pupil receives 45 separate 1-day fixed-period exclusions, or one 45-day fixed-period exclusion. This total applies across schools.[44]

David moves from School A to School B in March. At the point when he left School A, he had been excluded for a total of 43 days since the start of the academic year. If David commits a disciplinary offence meriting a fixed-period exclusion at School B at any point during the remainder of the academic year, the maximum fixed-period exclusion that School B can impose is 2 days.

A fixed-period exclusion does not have to be for a continuous period. Furthermore, a school can exclude a pupil for parts of the school day rather than a full day (for example, a lunchtime exclusion, which counts as half a school day).

So far as the duration of a fixed-period exclusion is concerned, in *R (on the application of K) v Headteacher and Governors of Tamworth Manor*

---

movement, DfE statutory guidance, August 2024, para 20

44 School Discipline (Pupil Exclusions and Reviews) (England) Regulations 2012, regulation 4 and 22.

High School[45], a 16-day fixed-period exclusion was found not to be a disproportionate or excessive penalty for a pupil who had indecently exposed himself, bringing his school into disrepute, and who had received numerous exclusions previously. The DfE guidance then in force suggested that an exclusion of one to three days was '*long enough to secure the benefits of exclusion without adverse educational consequences*'. This was found to be wholly inadequate given the nature and seriousness of the pupil's misconduct. The DfE guidance was subsequently updated and no longer recommends any particular length of fixed-period exclusion. However, it does indicate that where a pupil has received multiple exclusions, or is approaching the 45-day limit referred to above, the head teacher should consider whether exclusion is proving an effective sanction.[46]

Giving notice of exclusion to interested parties

The head teacher must inform the governing board of a fixed-period exclusion without delay where the pupil will be excluded for a total of more than 5 days in any term, or where the pupil will lose an opportunity to take a public examination or National Curriculum test.[47]

The head teacher must take account of their legal duty of care when sending a pupil home following an exclusion, whether permanent or fixed-period. The head teacher must also take reasonable steps without delay to notify the "relevant person", who may be the parent of the pupil, or the pupil himself if they are over 18 years old, the governing board, or

---

45 [2004] All ER (D) 45 (Nov)

46 Suspension and Permanent Exclusion from maintained schools, academies and pupil referral units in England, including pupil movement, DfE statutory guidance, August 2024, para 7

47 School Discipline (Pupil Exclusions and Reviews) Regulations 2012, regulation 5(2)–(3)

the local authority (or if applicable the home local authority) of the exclusion.

The notice given to the parent of a pupil must contain the following information:[48]

- the period of the exclusion and whether or not it is permanent,
- the reasons for the exclusion.
- the parents' right to make representations about the exclusion to the governing board, how representations should be made, how the pupil may be involved in this, and arrangements around any meeting where the governing board is legally required to consider the exclusion (as to which see Chapter 3).
- If the pupil is of compulsory school age, the notice should warn parents that they are under a duty not to allow their child to attend school or to be present in a public place at any time during school hours, and state the days upon which they must ensure this (without delay, and at the latest by the end of the afternoon session).[49] Penalty notices may be issued where parents allow their child to be present in a public place during school hours

48 under section 104 of the Education and Inspections Act 2006

49 Sections 103 to 105 of the Education and Inspections Act 2006. Failing to comply with this duty, without reasonable justification, is an offence prosecutable by a local authority. The maximum penalty on summary conviction is a fine not exceeding level 3 on the standard scale (up to £1,000). The local authority may issue a penalty notice rather than instituting formal proceedings. For more information, see the DfE's statutory guidance on school attendance: *School attendance parental responsibilities measures – statutory guidance for local authorities, school leaders, school staff, governing bodies and the police* (January 2015)

without reasonable justification during the first five days of a fixed period or permanent exclusion.

- If alternative provision is being provided, the start date, start and finish times, address and to whom the pupil should report on the first day should also be provided. If this cannot be provided by the end of the afternoon session, a subsequent notice may be issued with this information, without delay and not less than 48 hours before the alternative provision is due to start. If the head teacher fails to meet the deadline, they must still serve the notice; it is not invalid purely because it is delivered late.

Notice must usually be in writing. Parents may now be given an exclusion notice electronically if they have provided written consent for notice to be sent this way. Otherwise, written notification should be delivered directly to the parents; left at their usual or last-known home address; or posted to that address. Ideally, notification should be provided in person or by telephone in the first instance to allow for any initial questions or concerns. Information provided to parents must be clear and easily understood, including translation where required.

If the child is excluded for a further fixed period, or is subsequently permanently excluded, the head teacher must inform the parents without delay and must issue a new notice.

When notifying parents about an exclusion, the guidance also says that head teachers should draw attention to various relevant sources of free and impartial information, including a link to the statutory guidance itself. For a range of advice lines and other resources, please see the list at the back of this book.

Education during exclusion

The governing board (or, where the pupil has been excluded from a PRU, the local authority) must arrange suitable, full-time education for any pupil of compulsory school age for any fixed-period exclusion of more than 5 school days.[50] Where a pupil receives consecutive fixed-period exclusions, these are regarded as a cumulative period of exclusion for the purposes of this duty. This means that if a pupil has six or more consecutive school days of exclusion, then education must be arranged from the sixth school day of exclusion, regardless of whether this is as a result of one fixed-period or more than one fixed-period exclusion.

Returning to school/early intervention

Both parents and schools should be aware that a fixed-period exclusion is a warning sign: it suggests unusually serious misconduct and must be taken seriously. In many cases of permanent exclusion, there is a prior history of persistent disruptive behaviour and often at least one if not multiple fixed-period exclusions. In such cases, the DfE strongly advises schools to bear in mind the importance of looking behind the behaviour exhibited by the pupil to see whether they might have unmet needs.[51] Where a school has concerns about the behaviour, or risk of suspension and permanent exclusion, of a pupil with SEN, a disability, or an EHC plan it should, in partnership with others (including where relevant, the local authority), consider what additional support or alternative placement may be required. This should involve assessing the suitability of provision for a pupil's SEN or disability.

Schools should already have robust systems in place for reviewing their behaviour policy with a view to fostering early intervention for pupils who are struggling: see Chapter 1. Persistent disruptive behaviour may be a sign of underlying SEN and/or disabilities (as to which see Chapter

50 Education and Inspections Act 2006, section 100; Education Act 1996, section 19; Education (Provision of Full-Time Education for Excluded Pupils) (England) Regulations 2007, as amended by the Education (Provision of Full-Time Education for Excluded Pupils) (England) (Amendment) Regulations 2014

51 Suspension and Permanent Exclusion from maintained schools, academies and pupil referral units in England, including pupil movement, DfE statutory guidance, August 2024, para 56

6), or of emotional vulnerability (including, but not only, pupils in the care system; pupils known to their local authorities as children in need; and pupils with known child protection issues). Early intervention to mitigate the risk of exclusion is encouraged. This could include specialist teaching; any early help initiatives available via the child's local authority for children who may be at risk of permanent exclusion; CAMHS; or other agencies or services in the area. Where needs are identified, the school should take reasonable steps to meet those needs, prior to a decision to permanently exclude.

Schools are expected to have a strategy for reintegrating a pupil who returns to school following a fixed-period exclusion, and for managing their future behaviour. Schools should organise a reintegration meeting to help a pupil return to the school environment. This should be seen by both the parents (and/or pupil) and the school as an opportunity to devise strategies for future behaviour management and, where the pupil's needs so indicate,[52] the involvement of appropriate professionals and outside agencies. The reintegration meeting can also be used to arrange help for others within the school who may find the prospect of the pupil's return difficult, particularly if they have been harmed by that pupil. It may be appropriate, for instance, to ask the school's SEN coordinator, designated safeguarding lead and/or a local authority representative to attend the meeting. Parents, of course, should always be invited to reintegration meetings.

In order to ensure that the pupil returns to school with a full understanding of what expectations are in place around their behaviour and what support will be available, a reintegration meeting should, if possible, be held before the fixed-period exclusion ends and the child returns to school (but note that it would not be lawful to extend a fixed-period exclusion to accommodate a meeting if it cannot be held before

---

52 Suspension and Permanent Exclusion from maintained schools, academies and pupil referral units in England, including pupil movement, DfE statutory guidance, August 2024, para 31

the exclusion ends; in these circumstances the correct thing to do would be to arrange the meeting for the morning of the pupil's first day back).

Recording fixed-period exclusions / suspensions

Fixed-period exclusions must be formally recorded. The law requires all schools including independent schools to have an admission register and, with the exception of schools where all pupils are boarders, an attendance register. All pupils (regardless of their age) must be placed on both registers. The proprietor of a school who fails to comply with these regulations is guilty of an offence and can be fined.[53]

Schools must take the attendance register at the start of the first session of each school day and once during the second session. On each occasion, they must record whether every pupil is: *Present; Attending an approved educational activity (which includes alternative provision); Absent; or, Unable to attend due to exceptional circumstances.*[54] The school must identify the correct code to use before entering it on to the school's electronic register, or management information system which is used to download data to the School Census.

For school exclusions, schools must use Code E: *Excluded but no alternative provision made*. If no alternative provision is made for a pupil to continue their education whilst they are excluded but still on the admission register, they should be marked absent in the attendance register using Code E.

---

53 Education Act 1996, section 434(6)

54 Alternative provision here means the provision of suitable full-time education to those who would not otherwise receive it, including education for excluded pupils by local authorities; education arranged by schools for pupils from day 6 of a fixed-period exclusion; and pupils being directed by schools to off-site provision to improve their behaviour under section 29A of the Education Act 2002.

As set out above, suitable full-time education must be arranged for each excluded pupil from the sixth consecutive day of any fixed period or permanent exclusion. Where alternative provision is made, the pupil should be marked using the appropriate attendance code (Code B: Present at an Approved Off-Site Educational Activity).

Any exclusion of a pupil, even for short periods of time, must be formally recorded, as set out above.

Challenging a fixed-period exclusion

In this section, we look at the circumstances in which a parent or pupil can challenge a fixed-period exclusion.

Where the exclusion is a fixed-period exclusion *and* would bring the pupil's total number of school days of exclusion to more than 15 in a term, the governing board **must** consider reinstating the pupil within 15 school days of receiving notice of the exclusion.[55] Where the exclusion would result in the pupil missing a public examination or national curriculum test, the governing board **must** consider reinstating the pupil before the date of the examination of the test (so far as reasonably practicable) and in any event within 15 school days of receiving notice of the exclusion.[56]

Where the pupil has been excluded for more than 5 but less than 15 school days in the term, **and** where the parents make representations, the governing board must consider whether the excluded pupil should be reinstated within 50 days of receiving the notice of exclusion. If the parents do not make representations, the governing board is not required

55 The School Discipline (Pupil Exclusions and Reviews) (England) Regulations 2012, regulation 5. If the pupil has been permanently excluded, this means the home authority of the pupil too.

56 The School Discipline (Pupil Exclusions and Reviews) (England) Regulations 2012, regulation 5. If the pupil has been permanently excluded, this means the home authority of the pupil too.

to meet and cannot direct reinstatement. In addition to this, the head teacher must give notice in writing to the relevant person of the period of the exclusion and the reasons for it (that being the pupil's parent if they are under 18, or the pupil themselves if they are over 18). The notice must include information about how the parents or pupil can make representations about the decision to the governing board. This includes the means by which representations may be made and where and to whom representations should be sent. It should also state, where a meeting of the governing board is to consider the exclusion, that the relevant person may attend and be represented at the meeting (at their own expense),[57] and may be accompanied by a friend. It must also state that where the pupil is not the relevant person, the pupil may also be involved in the process of making representations, and set out how the pupil may be involved. [58]

The governing board's meeting

Arrangements for meetings of the governing board's disciplinary committee to consider fixed-period exclusions are the same as for a permanent exclusion, and are discussed in detail in Chapter 3.

Where the pupil will have returned to school before the governing board's meeting

In some circumstances, the pupil may already have returned to school by the time the governing board meets. In these circumstances, the governing board must still consider whether the pupil should be officially reinstated, and must not be tempted to rubber-stamp the head teacher's decision because they are of the view that it would make no practical

---

57 Any expense in connection with the representation of the relevant person is treated as the expense of the relevant person, rather than the school or local authority.

58 The School Discipline (Pupil Exclusions and Reviews) (England) Regulations 2012, regulation 6

difference to reinstate. The decision is not academic simply because the fixed-period exclusion has ended. The parents are likely to be concerned about the possible impact on their child's record of a fixed-term exclusion in terms of their future academic career and the schools available to their child in the event that they decide to move their child to a different school. The governors must make their decision on the merits of the decision to impose a fixed-period exclusion without regard to the fact that it has already ended.

Further routes of challenge

If the governing board upholds the fixed-period exclusion, there is no appeal against that decision to the Independent Review Panel. The Independent Review Panel only considers permanent exclusion. However, if the fixed-period exclusion was tainted by discrimination, it may be possible to bring a claim for discrimination in the First-tier Tribunal (for disability discrimination claims) or the County Court (for other forms of discrimination) (see Chapter 6). In theory, it may also be possible to bring a claim for judicial review (see Chapter 4), although this would be very unusual.

Screening, search and confiscation

Screening

Schools can require pupils to undergo screening (without physical contact) by a walk-through or hand-held metal detector, even if they do not have reasonable grounds to suspect that they have a weapon, and regardless of whether or not the pupils consent.[59] Any member of school staff can conduct the screening. The school cannot use force to compel a pupil to go through the metal detector. The DfE advice is that schools are entitled to make entry to the premises conditional upon screening,

[59] Arguably falls within the head teacher's determination of the behaviour policy under section 89 Education and Inspections Act 2006

and to refuse to admit a pupil who refuses to be screened. They are also entitled to mark the pupil's absence as unauthorised if the reason for the pupil's absence is that the pupil refused to undergo screening.[60]

Pupils have a right to a reasonable level of respect for their private life under Article 8 of the European Convention on Human Rights. However, this right is not unqualified: a public body may interfere with this right, provided that the interference is a proportionate means of achieving a legitimate aim. The DfE's view is that screening pupils using a non-intrusive form of screening that involves no physical contact is a proportionate means of ensuring the safety of staff, pupils and visitors and therefore a justified interference with Article 8 rights. 61The head teacher should oversee the school's practice of searching to ensure that a culture of safe, proportionate and appropriate searching is maintained, which safeguards the welfare of all pupils and staff with support from the designated safeguarding lead (or deputy).

Search and confiscation at common law

Schools have the power at common law to search pupils for any item with the pupil's consent. Formal written consent is not required – it is sufficient for the teacher to ask the pupil to turn out their pockets, or if they can look in the pupil's bag, and for the pupil to agree.[62] If the pupil has an item in their bag which is banned under school rules, the teacher has the power to confiscate it under the general power to discipline described above. This includes the power to confiscate, retain or dispose of a pupil's property as a sanction, as long as it is reasonable to do so in

---

60 *Searching, screening and confiscation: Advice for headteachers, school staff and governing bodies*, DfE departmental advice, July 2022 for further guidance on this.

61 *Searching, screening and confiscation: Advice for headteachers, school staff and governing bodies*, DfE departmental advice, July 2022, page 6

62 *Searching, screening and confiscation: Advice for headteachers, school staff and governing bodies*, DfE departmental advice, July 2022 para 28

the circumstances. Teachers are protected from liability for loss of, or damage to, confiscated items, provided that the decision to confiscate was lawful (whether under the general power to discipline in section 91 or otherwise).

If items are banned at school, the school must make this clear, and set out which items are banned, in its behaviour policy and its communications with parents and pupils.

If a pupil refuses to agree to be searched for a banned item (unless it is a prohibited item, discussed below), the teacher cannot carry out the search against the pupil's will. Nor can the teacher use force, reasonable or otherwise. The teacher can, however, impose an appropriate sanction as set out in the behaviour policy. Again, the behaviour policy should be clear as to the consequences if a pupil refuses to consent to a search.[63]

<u>Statutory power to carry out search with or without pupil's consent for prohibited items</u>

Head teachers, and other staff so authorised by the head teacher, also have a statutory power to search without consent for certain "prohibited items". There is no requirement to seek parental consent to the search, or to inform the pupil's parents before a search takes place. Nor is there an express requirement to make or keep a record of the search, although our view is that it would be sensible to do so.

The extent of the search is limited: pupils may be required to remove outer clothing, but the power does not extend to the removal of clothing immediately over underwear or worn next to the skin.

63 *Searching, screening and confiscation: Advice for headteachers, school staff and governing bodies*, DfE departmental advice, July 2022, paras 18–23 and para 56

List of prohibited items

Staff may only conduct a search without consent where they have reasonable grounds to suspect that the pupil may have one of the following prohibited items in their possession:[64]

- Knives and weapons
- Alcohol
- Illegal drugs
- Stolen goods
- Tobacco/cigarette papers
- Fireworks
- Pornographic images
- Any item that the member of staff reasonably suspects has been or is likely to be used to commit an offence, personal injury or property damage
- Any item banned by the school rules which has been identified in the rules as an item which may be searched for. It is important to note that this does not permit teachers to search for an item that is banned but is not identified as banned within the school rules.

64 Education Act 1996, section 550ZA(3)

Disposal of prohibited items found during a search

There are specific rules about whether and how to pass to the police, retain or dispose of each category of prohibited item.[65] In summary, weapons, knives and extreme child pornography must always be handed over to the police as soon as practicable. Illegal drugs must be passed to the police as soon as possible, unless the member of staff thinks that there is a good reason to dispose of them. Otherwise, the teacher has some discretion as to what to do with the items in question, but should not return the item to the pupil.

Power to view data or files on electronic devices seized during a search for prohibited items

Note that if an electronic device (e.g. a telephone) that is prohibited by school rules or which the member of staff suspects has been or is likely to be used to commit an offence, personal injury or property damage, is found during a search for prohibited items, the searcher may examine any data or files on the device where there is good reason to do so; they may also delete data or files if they think that there is a good reason to do so, unless they intend to pass the device to the police. Neither pupil nor parental consent is required if the device has been seized in a lawful search and is a prohibited item as defined above.

Reasonable grounds for search required

Although pupil consent is not required for a search for prohibited items, the member of staff must have reasonable grounds for suspecting that the pupil may have a prohibited item in their possession. The search must be carried out on school premises (or, if off the premises, where the member of staff has lawful charge of the pupil). Reasonable grounds could include a pupil behaving in a way that suggested concealment, or overhearing the pupil or other pupils discussing the item, but it is really up to the member

---

65 Education Act 1996, section 550ZC

of staff to decide whether they have reasonable grounds for carrying out a search.

The pupil's Article 8 right to respect for their private life is relevant in this context too. The DfE's view is that the powers to search for and seize prohibited items from a pupil in the Education Act 1996 are, if complied with, compatible with Article 8 (i.e. they represent a justified interference with the pupil's right to privacy).[66]

Requirements as to persons present during search

The search must be carried out in the presence of the pupil, by a person of the same sex as the pupil being searched, and in the presence of a witness who, if possible, should also be of the same sex as the pupil being searched. The only exception to these three requirements is where the searcher reasonably believes that there is a risk of serious harm being caused to a person if the search is not conducted immediately, and where it is not reasonably practicable to summon another member of staff.[67]

Use of reasonable force when searching for prohibited items

Members of staff can use such force as is reasonable given the circumstances when conducting a search for a prohibited item (unless the search is for an item identified as banned by the school rules: staff may not use force, reasonable or otherwise, in conducting a search for this category of prohibited item). The power to use reasonable force more generally in situations involving pupils is discussed later on in this chapter.

---

66 *Searching, screening and confiscation: Advice for headteachers, school staff and governing bodies*, DfE departmental advice, July 2022, page 6

67 *Searching, screening and confiscation: Advice for headteachers, school staff and governing bodies*, DfE departmental advice, July 2022, para 25–27, para 32

Misconduct outside of school

Pupils may be disciplined for misbehaving outside of the school premises "*to such an extent as is reasonable*",[68] although the decision as to sanction must take place on school premises. The behaviour policy should clearly set out what the school will do in response to misconduct which occurs outside the school premises and is either witnessed by a staff member or reported to the school. This should include the sanctions that will be imposed. If the behaviour policy so permits, pupils may be disciplined for behaviour that takes place whilst the pupil is:[69]

- Taking part in any school-organised or school-related activity off-site
- Travelling to or from school
- Wearing school uniform
- Otherwise capable of being identified as a pupil of the school

Members of staff may also discipline a pupil if none of the above apply, where the pupil's misbehaviour could

- have repercussions for the orderly running of the school
- pose a threat to another pupil or member of the public, or
- adversely affect the reputation of the school.

The behaviour policy should be as clear as possible about the circumstances in which sanctions may be imposed for conduct that took

68 Education and Inspections Act 2006 section 90

69 *Behaviour and discipline in schools: Advice for head teachers and school* staff, DfE departmental advice, February 2024, page 25–26

place off school premises, so that teachers understand what their powers are, and so that pupils and parents fully understand the consequences of misbehaviour off the premises.

Use of reasonable force by staff

All members of school staff, including unpaid volunteers or parents accompanying students who have been temporarily put in charge of students by the head teacher, have the power to use reasonable force to

- prevent pupils from committing an offence
- prevent pupils from injuring themselves
- prevent pupils from injuring others or damaging property
- maintain good order and discipline in the classroom

As set out previously, head teachers and specifically authorised staff also have the power to use reasonable force to exercise the statutory power to search for prohibited items.

Parental consent is not required in order to use lawful and reasonable force. Nor is there any specific requirement to inform parents that reasonable force has been used in relation to their child, although the DfE recommends that parents are informed of serious incidents involving the use of force.[70]

The school's behaviour policy should include the power to use reasonable force. There is no requirement to have a policy regarding the use of force, but it is good practice to set out the circumstances in which force might

70 *Use of reasonable force: advice for headteachers, staff and governing bodies*, July 2013: DfE departmental advice, page 7

be used. The school must take into account its duty to make reasonable adjustments for disabled pupils (which is likely to include pupils with SEN, especially those who have an EHC Plan in place: see Chapter 6). This is particularly the case in relation to pupils with disabilities that prevent them from being able to calm down without appropriate strategies which may include physical restraint. It is important that the school's behaviour policy is as clear as possible about the circumstances in which reasonable and lawful force might be used.

The DfE says that reasonable force covers "*the broad range of actions used by most teachers at some point in their career that involve a degree of physical contact with pupils*", from taking a pupil's arm to move them to safety, to intervening in fights or restraining a pupil to prevent injury. Reasonable force means using no more force than is needed in the particular circumstances at issue. Obviously, staff should always try to avoid causing injury.[71]

The DfE advises that force in the educational setting will be used to control (for example, blocking a pupil's path) or restrain (physically holding back a pupil or bringing them under control).[72] Situations in which reasonable force might be appropriate could include[73]

- Removing disruptive children from the classroom after they have refused to obey an instruction to leave

- Preventing a pupil from behaving in a way that disrupts a school event, trip or visit

---

71 *Use of reasonable force: advice for headteachers, staff and governing bodies*, July 2013: DfE departmental advice, page 4

72 *Use of reasonable force: advice for headteachers, staff and governing bodies*, July 2013: DfE departmental advice, page 4

73 *Use of reasonable force: advice for headteachers, staff and governing bodies*, July 2013: DfE departmental advice, page 5

- Preventing a pupil from leaving a classroom, where otherwise the pupil might be put in danger, or disrupt the behaviour of others
- Preventing a pupil from attacking another member of staff or pupil
- Stopping a fight
- Restraining a pupil who is in danger of harming themselves.

Using force as a sanction is always unlawful and will never be considered reasonable.

Use of social media/Internet/IT

Misbehaviour and cyberbullying online are, regrettably, becoming more and more common, and may occur both on and off school premises. This will likely increase in depth and difficulty as artificial intelligence takes hold in schools. Similarly, pupils may misuse IT facilities, e.g. searching for or viewing inappropriate content online whilst using school IT facilities, whether on or off the premises. Behaviour policies should expressly address the circumstances in which the use of social media and the Internet (including cyberbullying) may attract a disciplinary sanction, and which sanctions may be imposed; there should be clear cross-reference to any separate policy regarding IT and the use of social media/the Internet by pupils, on or off the premises.

Off-site direction by maintained schools to improve behaviour

Maintained schools have the power to direct a pupil off-site for education to improve their behaviour.[74] Academies cannot exercise this specific

[74] Education Act 2002, section 29A; see also *Alternative Provision: Statutory*

statutory power but can do so under their general powers as set out in their Trust's articles of association. The regulations and statutory guidance do not apply to Academies, but it would be sensible for them to follow the regulations and guidance as closely as possible. Directing off-site is sometimes referred to as "alternative provision", but it is important to note that "alternative provision" can be used in relation to a number of different means of providing full-time education to pupils who are for one reason or another unable to attend school (e.g. due to exclusion, illness, or otherwise, as well as being directed off site under section 29A).

This measure is often used when a pupil is at risk of permanent exclusion. The governing body of the pupil's school arranges an alternative placement off-site at which the pupil will receive educational provision, the objective being to improve the pupil's behaviour. The pupil remains on the roll of their school. The aim is for the pupil to transfer back from the alternative placement to their school (as opposed to managed moves, which the DfE suggests should be a permanent measure.

The measure is a requirement, not a voluntary process. It is not dependent upon consent from the pupil or their parents. However, the process should be collaborative, so far as possible. Regulations provide for a strict procedure and a strict timetable.[75] The transferring school must give the parents of the child (or the child themselves, if over 18) notice in writing, including the address of the alternative provision; the number of days for which the pupil is required to attend off site; the reasons for, and objectives of, imposing the requirement; and other information about the placement. The notice must be given as soon as practicable after the decision has been made, and not less than 2 school days before the first day of attendance off-site. The school must keep the alternative

guidance for local authorities, DfE statutory guidance, January 2013

75 Education (Educational Provision for Improving Behaviour) Regulations 2010, as amended by the Education (Educational Provision for Improving Behaviour) (Amendment) Regulations 2012

placement under review by holding a review meeting and there is a strict timetable for this process.

Directing a child to attend a different placement, away from their familiar setting, peers and teachers, can sometimes be seen as draconian and should only be used where it is absolutely necessary. Parents may be concerned that their school is using this arrangement to remove their child rather than put appropriate interventions in place in school to resolve issues around behaviour. This is particularly the case for parents of children with SEN or disabilities, who will be particularly vigilant for any sign that the placement is being used to downplay the fact that the pupil is not in the right type of setting.

Conclusion

The behaviour policy will be of critical importance whenever an exclusion is challenged. Schools are expected to ensure that their behaviour policy is followed by staff across the school day, and to adjust it in respect of individual pupils with disabilities so far as is reasonable (see Chapter 6). Obviously, there is a substantial degree of discretion for the class teacher addressing minor acts of misconduct during a lesson, although care must be taken to ensure that sanctions are fair, merited, and not discriminatory. But any head teacher deciding whether or not to permanently exclude a pupil must review the school's behaviour policy and the pupil's disciplinary history with great care, and consider whether any intervention or measure short of exclusion remains that could be taken that has not been taken. This is discussed further in Chapter 2. Head teachers should be particularly careful in considering exclusion of looked-after pupils and pupils who have a disability, or who are showing distinct signs of having a disability that affects their behaviour. There is more discussion regarding the latter in Chapter 6.

In summary:

- Schools are under a duty to put in place and maintain behaviour policies.
- Behaviour policies cannot provide for every possible scenario, and should not be so prescriptive that they fetter the discretion of teachers and staff to do what is right in a particular situation. However, they should address a wide range of issues relevant to behaviour rather than mechanically rehearsing offences and sanctions, and ensure that pupils and parents know what is expected in terms of behaviour, and what the likely sanctions are for misconduct.
- Parents challenging an exclusion should look carefully at the school's behaviour policy against the disciplinary history and the decision-making leading up to the decision to exclude.
- Technical failures by the school to follow its behaviour policy that would have made no difference to the outcome may be disregarded by the Independent Review Panel and/or any subsequent court reviewing the exclusion. However, schools should follow their behaviour policy at all times, and ensure that the disciplinary history and behaviour policy are carefully reviewed by the Head before a decision to exclude is taken – or risk a finding that a permanent exclusion was unlawful, or worse still discriminatory.

Further reading

In this chapter we have referred to various published DfE statutory guidance and departmental advice in relation to school discipline. These are:

- *Behaviour and discipline in schools: guidance for governing bodies*, DfE statutory guidance, July 2013. Statutory guidance to which governing bodies must have regard when making and reviewing their written statement of general principles to guide the head teacher, and when guiding the head teacher as to their wish to include or address certain measures in the policy.

- *Behaviour and discipline in schools: advice for head teachers and school staff*, DfE departmental advice, February 2024. Non-statutory advice on developing a school behaviour policy and the power of members of staff to discipline pupils for misconduct.

- *Use of reasonable force: advice for headteachers, staff and governing bodies*, DfE departmental advice, July 2013. Non-statutory departmental advice on the use of force in schools for governing bodies, head teachers and school staff.

- *Searching, screening and confiscation: advice for schools*, DfE departmental advice, July 2022. Non-statutory departmental advice on the powers that are available to schools to screen and search pupils.

- *Alternative Provision: Statutory guidance for local authorities*, DfE statutory guidance, January 2013. Statutory guidance on the provision of suitable full-time education to those who would not otherwise receive it, including education for excluded pupils by local authorities; education arranged by schools for pupils from day 6 of a fixed-period exclusion; and pupils being directed by schools to off-site provision to improve their behaviour.

See Chapter 6 for additional resources that may be of interest where discrimination is a concern.

CHAPTER TWO

THE DECISION TO PERMANENTLY EXCLUDE: MAINTAINED SCHOOLS, PUPIL REFERRAL UNITS AND ACADEMIES

Introduction and overview

The Education Act 2011 reformed school exclusions procedure by inserting section 51A into the Education Act 2002.[76] Section 51A (1) allows head teachers of maintained schools,[77] principals of Academies and teachers in charge of pupil referral units ("PRUs") to issue fixed-period (suspensions) or permanent exclusions. We looked at fixed-period exclusions (suspensions) in Chapter 1. In this chapter, we look at the circumstances in which a pupil can be permanently excluded from a maintained school, academy, or pupil referral unit.

Since these are the most severe sanctions available to schools, there is also a statutory scheme which regulates the circumstances in which these sanctions can be imposed, and provides for review of fixed-period exclusions and permanent exclusions, set out in regulations made under section 51A.[78] This scheme applies to all maintained schools,

---

76 Education Act 2011, section 4

77 This means a community, foundation or voluntary school, a community or foundation special school or a maintained nursery school – Education Act 2002, section 1(3), as inserted by the Education and Inspections Act 2006, section 1(4).

78 School Discipline (Pupil Exclusions and Reviews) (England) Regulations

academies,[79] alternative provision academies[80] and PRUs, and is explored in Chapter 3. It does not, however, apply to independent schools; the position in relation to independent schools is summarised in Chapter 5.

The latest version of the Department for Education's statutory guidance, *Suspension and Permanent Exclusion from maintained schools, academies and pupil referral units in England, including pupil movement*, as at the date of this publication, is the August 2024 edition.

Permanent exclusion is a sanction of last resort. The effects of permanent exclusion upon excluded pupils are far-reaching and, in many cases, lifelong, as described in the Introduction. In particular, head teachers should avoid, so far as possible, the permanent exclusion of any pupil with an Education, Health and Care Plan, or looked-after children.

Where there is an allegation of discrimination (under the Equality Act 2010) in relation to a fixed-period or permanent exclusion, parents can also make a claim to the First-tier Tribunal (Special Educational Needs and Disability) for disability discrimination, or to the County Court for other forms of discrimination. Chapter 6 explores issues relating to disability discrimination and other forms of discrimination in the context of exclusions.

Who can exclude?

In the maintained school and academy context, only head teachers of maintained schools, teachers in charge of PRUs and principals of Academy schools and alternative provision Academies can exclude a pupil.[81] If a head teacher is absent from school, the person acting up in

---

2012

79 Including free schools, studio schools and university technology colleges

80 Including alternative provision free schools

81 Education Act 2002, section 51A

this position during their absence may exclude a pupil.[82] An acting head teacher is someone appointed to carry out the functions of the head teacher in the head teacher's absence or pending the appointment of a head teacher. This will not necessarily be the deputy head teacher: it will depend upon who is appointed to the role of acting head teacher.

In an academy, 'principal' includes acting principal by virtue of regulation 21 of the School Discipline (Pupil Exclusions and Reviews) (England) Regulations 2012.

The importance of early intervention

Permanent exclusion is a sanction of last resort. In some cases the pupil involved will not previously have been in any trouble and will have been excluded due to a one-off incident of extreme seriousness. In other cases, a permanent exclusion is the culmination of a long period of persistent disruptive behaviour by the pupil in question. In the latter situation, the permanent exclusion may have been preceded by one or more fixed-period exclusions. Persistent disruptive behaviour may be a sign of underlying SEN or disabilities (as to which see Chapter 6), or of emotional vulnerability (including, but not only, pupils in the care system; pupils known to their local authorities as children in need; and pupils with known child protection issues) or a sign of sexual abuse or peer-on-peer bullying.

As set out in Chapter 1, part of the school's strategy for early intervention should be a robust system for review of the behaviour policy to ensure that parents and pupils understand it, that it is fit for purpose, that there are systems in place to identify struggling pupils and that the behaviour policy is not discriminatory.

---

82 Education Act 1996, section 579; "head teacher" includes acting head teacher.

In cases of persistent disruptive behaviour, early intervention to mitigate the risk of exclusion is encouraged. The statutory guidance emphasises the importance of looking behind the behaviour exhibited by the pupil to see whether they might have unmet needs (which could include SEN, mental health or difficulties at home) and of taking appropriate action.[83] This could include greater pastoral support such as access to counselling, mentoring or buddying; a multi-agency assessment; specialist teaching; any early help initiatives available via the child's local authority for children who may be at risk of permanent exclusion; CAMHS intervention; speech and language therapist input; occupational therapist input; or other agencies or services in the area.

Where needs are identified, the school should take reasonable steps to meet those needs, prior to a decision to permanently exclude.

> *Eliza is becoming increasingly rude to her teachers and lacks concentration and effort in the classroom, for which she receives multiple detentions. After seeing a pattern emerge, her teachers seek advice from the school's SENCo to see whether Eliza might have any hidden learning needs. The SENCo speaks with Eliza's carers, who agree to a local authority educational psychologist assessment. This assessment reveals that Eliza has severe dyslexia, which causes her difficulties and frustration in the classroom. The school then puts in place dyslexia-specific support for Eliza, and the number of detentions that Eliza receives decreases. The school has adequately explored the causes of her deteriorating behaviour and mitigated the risk of permanent exclusion.*

---

83 *Suspension and Permanent Exclusion from maintained schools, academies and pupil referral units in England, including pupil movement Guidance for maintained schools, academies, and pupil referral units in England* DfE statutory guidance, August 2024

The Investigation stage

When the head teacher is notified that an incident has occurred which is potentially serious enough to merit exclusion, they must ensure that a full investigation is undertaken. It is essential that their decision is based upon a clear understanding of what happened, and what aggravating and mitigating factors might have been at play. This will involve gathering as much evidence as is possible about the offence itself, as well as all of the relevant information available about the pupil. We list some factors that are likely to be relevant later in this chapter.

In some cases there will be little dispute as to the underlying facts. In other cases, the pupil may completely deny any wrongdoing. Or they may offer an alternative or competing account which, if accepted, would mean that the conduct was less serious or more understandable than it appeared. In these circumstances head teachers must conduct an investigation, gather evidence, and come to a conclusion about what actually happened; they must then consider the appropriate sanction (if a sanction is merited).

The test of whether a particular case is so serious that a permanent exclusion is necessary is set out later in this chapter. It is important that the decision to exclude is not made in the heat of the moment.

<u>Who investigates?</u>

The head teacher does not need to carry out the investigation themselves, as long as it is they who take the decision whether or not to exclude. If practicable, it is sensible for the primary investigator to be someone who has not previously been involved in the incidents, although depending upon the scale of the incident and the size of the school this may not be possible.

Records kept by the school

Head teachers should obviously consult any relevant records that have been kept by their school. Any tribunal scrutinising an exclusion – whether that is the Independent Review Panel (see Chapter 3), the County Court or First-tier Tribunal on a discrimination claim (see Chapter 6), or the High Court on a judicial review (see Chapter 4) – will expect the school to have kept reasonable records in relation to pupils' behaviour; sanctions imposed upon them; information of pastoral concern, such as illness, difficulties at home, bereavements, bullying, and anything else that might impact upon their ability to engage with the disciplinary policy or the curriculum; their academic and pastoral progress; and, of course, any SEN or disability and any reasonable adjustments made for them in that regard, or any EHC Plan that is maintained for them.

It is important to add that whilst keeping these records, and reviewing them carefully, is likely to be helpful and relevant to the decision whether or not to exclude, they are also likely to be important evidence in any subsequent review of the exclusion by the governing board and Independent Review Panel, as well as any subsequent discrimination claim.

Most schools – not necessarily all – now have access to internal information management software that enables them to record a vast amount of information, such as CPOMS. This will generally include a behaviour log for each pupil. Formats vary but generally speaking, the class teacher will be able to record, in the classroom, the brief details of an incident involving a pupil together with the sanction that was imposed or any follow-up (for example, some incidents may lead to a discussion with the school SENCO (Special Educational Needs Co-ordinator), safeguarding referral to the LA or liaison with another third party). It will then be possible to produce contemporaneous behaviour logs and logs of important interventions (if any) from this system.

As an aside, it is important for parents to be realistic about how much information will be recorded in relation to an incident that does not lead to a fixed-period or permanent exclusion. This can be a real difficulty in cases of persistent disruptive behaviour, where the head teacher may have taken a number of lower-level incidents into disruption over a period of time where there was a less comprehensive investigation. However, given that a teacher in a mainstream school is likely to have between 20 and 30+ pupils to manage at the same time as issuing a detention. The description of the incident is likely to be brief in those circumstances. However, it is reasonable to expect that any sanction given will be recorded on the behaviour log, and also that any reasonable adjustments will be recorded (e.g. that extra warnings were given to someone with a disability that affects their ability to process instructions).

Information systems may also generate automatic processes. For example, if a detention is imposed an automated text may be sent to parents informing them of the detention; if the pupil is marked as not attending a detention that was set then the system will automatically generate an alert to the parents; and so on.

If the school does not have an information system management like this, it should have some sort of system in place – even if it is writing entries in a book, so long as compliant with data protection legislation – for recording important events in relation to a student. At the very least, important decisions should be documented via letters, minutes or emails.

Our view is that a school can reasonably be expected to keep records in relation to:

- Reviews of the behaviour policy to ensure that it is fit for purpose and does not discriminate (see Chapter 1)
- Information as to the pupil's academic and pastoral progress
- Behavioural incidents and sanctions imposed

- Information as to any significant issues in the pupil's life of which the school is aware and which might affect the pupil's engagement generally within school: bereavements, parental separation or divorce, recent illness or time out of school for reasons not connected with disability (for example, a period of time out of school due to having broken a limb which has healed without difficulty and therefore is unlikely to give rise to an ongoing disability), a serious illness on the part of a close family member, and so on.

- Meetings with parents, particularly where behaviour, SEN or disability is discussed, even if it is only by way of a follow-up email recording what was agreed. Formal meetings or meetings in relation to significant events, such as reintegration meetings or early intervention meetings held because a pupil is considered to be at risk of permanent exclusion should be minuted.

- Information relating to a pupil's SEN and/or disability, including reports and information received relating to diagnosis, requests for or recommendations of reasonable adjustments (by parents or by professionals/experts) and reasonable adjustments made or not made, with reasons why

- Meetings with or liaison with third parties in relation to the pupil: safeguarding referrals, commissioned services such as Educational Psychology, Occupational Therapy, Speech and Language Therapy, specialist teaching services (ASD, VI, HI), CAMHS should all be recorded. Training received from the SENCO or third parties in relation to the pupil (e.g. in relation to the reasonable adjustments required or the EHC Plan in place) should also be recorded.

- Evidence that information regarding SEN or disability (e.g. EHC plan and/or agreed reasonable adjustments) or other important issues such as recent bereavement, family difficulties or other material factors likely to affect a pupil's behaviour or engagement with school life was disseminated promptly to staff – including teachers and TAs – working with the pupil

- School-wide training, e.g. INSET training, training from outside organisations such as the National Autism Society, British Dyslexia Association or similar. The school should be in a position to prove that all staff requiring the training attended, by having them confirm attendance or sign a register.

- The SENCO should review, and record their reviews, of provision being delivered to pupils with EHC Plans or reasonable adjustments in place. If, as sometimes happens, a teacher is not making reasonable adjustments that have been agreed, the SENCo should deal with this promptly and firmly, and record what happened and how it was resolved.

Collecting the evidence

The evidence of the breach, or breaches, of the school's behavioural policy needs to be:

- Formally recorded
- Taken from multiple sources – such as statements from all witnesses involved
- Of a legible quality
- Easy to understand
- Made available in an accessible format for the parents
- Redacted, if appropriate, but not to the extent that it makes following events difficult.

A thorough investigation will involve identifying all potential witnesses, including other pupils and staff. If the incident under investigation took place off site, consideration should be given to gathering evidence from third parties.

Investigators, and other staff assisting pupils with producing statements, must be aware of the sensitivity involved in taking accounts and witness statements from pupils. Pupils, particularly very young pupils, will not be familiar with giving formal accounts and are likely to be very anxious about getting into trouble themselves; about the effect of "telling tales" that may affect their relationships with other pupils; and about disappointing staff by giving the "wrong" account. Staff taking accounts from pupils must remain calm, avoiding any suggestion of aggression, disappointment, or frustration. Leading questions should be avoided ("did X hit Y?", "X was very angry, wasn't he?"), partly because they may mislead pupils into thinking that a particular "slant" is required, and partly because if it is clear that accounts were elicited via leading questions the impact of the witness's evidence may be diminished or extinguished altogether.

The evidence of each witness should be recorded in writing and signed by them if possible or otherwise confirmed by them (although failure to do so does not mean that they cannot be used in a subsequent review), so that they can be disclosed if a subsequent decision is challenged.

The evidence that the school may consider is not limited to witness evidence. CCTV and audio evidence may be used (schools should ensure that their policies cover any use of CCTV within the school, including in disciplinary investigations); there may also be physical evidence, such as items seized from the pupil or found in incriminating circumstances. Where the school's case rests largely or solely on physical evidence, and where the facts are in dispute, then the physical evidence, if practicable, should be retained and be available for the governors to see. Where there are difficulties in retaining physical evidence, photographs or signed witness statements should be used.

There have been some authorities on the nature and quality of investigations that resulted in decisions to exclude. In *R (Culkin) v Wirral IAP,*[84] the Court found that a school's investigation into the pupil's conduct was sufficient to identify serious and persistent conduct justifying permanent exclusion. The fact that some of the statements gathered from witnesses were not signed or dated did not render the process unfair; the weight to be put on the statements in light of the lack of signature and/or date was a matter for the Panel and the pupil and his parents had received sufficient information to understand the case against him.

In *R on the application of CR v Independent Review Panel of Lambeth*[85] the speed of the investigation was said to be surprising, but the governing board had been entitled to uphold the decision of the head teacher. In *R (Griffiths) v Lewisham College,*[86] the defendant college had failed to adhere to its own disciplinary procedures in connection with a permanent exclusion. The student had not, amongst other matters, been given the stipulated notice period, a clear, advance statement of the nature of the conduct complained of or a proper opportunity to dispute the facts relied upon. A subsequent appeal hearing did not cure these defects, as its scope of review was unduly limited.

Head teachers should keep detailed records of their investigation (or ensure that whoever investigates does so), the reasons for their decision to exclude, and the factors that were or were not taken into account.

Standard of proof

When establishing the facts in relation to alleged misconduct, the head teacher must apply the civil standard of proof; i.e. 'on the balance of probabilities' it is more likely than not that a fact is true, rather than the

84 [2009] ELR 287

85 [2014] EWHC 2461 (Admin)

86 [2007] EWHC 809 (Admin)

criminal standard of 'beyond reasonable doubt.'[87] This means that the head teacher should accept that something happened if it is more likely that it happened than that it did not happen. The more serious the nature of the allegation and thus the possible sanction, the more compelling the evidence necessary to support it is likely to need to be.[88]

Interim fixed-period exclusions pending investigation

There is no explicit power to impose an interim fixed-period exclusion (suspension) pending investigation. In the DfE's statutory guidance, all that is said is that in some exceptional cases usually where further evidence comes to light during a fixed-period exclusion, a further suspension may be issued to begin immediately after the first suspension, or a permanent exclusion may be issued to begin immediately after the end of the suspension.[89] The guidance is silent upon how further evidence might come to light.

For this reason, it is not clear what a head teacher may lawfully do if they have been unable to conclude the investigation on the day that the allegation comes to light. The head teacher may have been unable to speak to key witnesses or obtain key evidence; or may feel that further time is required to review the pupil's history. They may be aware that the

87 *Suspension and Permanent Exclusion from maintained schools, academies and pupil referral units in England, including pupil movement Guidance for maintained schools, academies, and pupil referral units in England* DfE statutory guidance, August 2024, paragraph 3; School Discipline (Pupil Exclusions and Reviews) (England) Regulations 2012, Regulation 9

88 See *R (S) v Governing Body of YP School [2004] ELR 37; R (H) v IAP for Y College* [2005] ELR 25; *R (Culkin) v Wirral IAP* [2009] ELR 287 and *R (S) v Head Teacher of Claremont High School* [2001] EWHC 488 (Admin) para 17

89 *Suspension and Permanent Exclusion from maintained schools, academies and pupil referral units in England, including pupil movement Guidance for maintained schools, academies, and pupil referral units in England* DfE statutory guidance, August 2024, paragraph 10

evidence they need to make a decision one way or the other will not be available for another day or so (for example, obtaining and viewing relevant CCTV or other real evidence in the hands of a third party). At the same time, the conduct alleged may be so serious that the head teacher may be concerned about the pupil or pupils accused of misconduct remaining on the premises pending the investigation.

If there is already sufficient evidence to justify a fixed-period exclusion (suspension) (see case study below) then it is likely to be lawful to do so, and to state in the notice that investigations continue and a further fixed-period or permanent exclusion may follow. Without such evidence, imposing a fixed-period exclusion pending further investigation may be unlawful, particularly if there were in fact measures that could have been taken internally to mitigate risk (e.g. keeping pupils apart or banning them from a specific area). Every measure should be taken to mitigate risk without imposing a penalty that might prove to be unwarranted. It may well be appropriate to take safeguarding advice.[90]

If the head teacher concludes that a fixed-period exclusion is required immediately, in our view the head teacher should include a statement that further investigations are to be carried out which may result in further information coming to light, and that for this reason it is possible that a further fixed-period exclusion or a permanent exclusion will be imposed to take effect immediately after the current fixed-period exclusion expires. If this is not made clear in the notice, parents and pupils may be forgiven for assuming that the fixed-term exclusion is the final sanction for the misconduct alleged, and the head teacher will face difficult questions in any subsequent challenge about why the position was not made clear.

---

90 See, for example, the advice on internal management and action to be taken following allegations of sexual harassment: Keeping children safe in education 2024: Statutory guidance for schools and colleges, part 5

Any further exclusion, whether fixed-period or permanent, must be the subject of a new decision and a new notice (the head teacher's obligations in relation to notifying others of decisions to exclude is set out later in this chapter). It is unlawful for a fixed-period exclusion to be extended beyond the term originally fixed, or to "convert" a fixed-period exclusion previously issued into a permanent exclusion without there being exceptional circumstances usually where further evidence has come to light.

> *Paddy, a sixth former, and Boris, who is in Year 11, are caught drinking alcohol on school premises. The school's behaviour policy says that drinking alcohol on the premises will attract an immediate suspension. Margot, one of their classmates, has told the head teacher that Paddy is well known for obtaining alcohol for younger pupils. If this is correct, it is likely to result in Paddy's permanent exclusion under the behaviour policy, which prohibits the supply of prohibited substances (defined to include alcohol) on school premises. The head teacher issues notice of suspension in respect of Boris and Paddy. In the notice relating to Paddy, he adds that he is still investigating further issues relating to the supply of the alcohol, and that if further evidence comes to light in relation to this Paddy is at risk of a further suspension or permanent exclusion.*

<u>Police involvement and parallel criminal proceedings</u>

In some cases, the pupil's misconduct may lead to police involvement and the institution of parallel criminal proceedings. The pupil may feel that the head teacher should await the outcome of such proceedings before deciding whether or not to exclude. There is no obligation upon the head teacher to do so. In such circumstances, the head teacher may make a decision on the evidence available to them on the balance of probabilities as to what happened, and impose a penalty accordingly.

Whether or not it is appropriate to investigate and impose a sanction pending the resolution of parallel proceedings in an individual case will depend upon the circumstances and must be considered on a case-by-case basis by the head teacher. There is no one rule that fits all situations. In some cases there may be a risk that action taken by the head teacher would prejudice the police investigation and/or any subsequent or ongoing prosecution. Alternatively, there may be circumstances which would render it unreasonable for the head teacher to make a decision about what happened whilst an independent investigation covering the same circumstances is ongoing. Careful liaison with the police and/or local children's social services will assist the head teacher in whether or not action is appropriate or whether they should wait. The head teacher should also consult the designated safeguarding lead (or a deputy) in appropriate cases, such as those involving physical or sexual violence.

Where the evidence is limited by a police investigation or criminal proceedings (for example, critical evidence is held by the police and cannot be considered or examined), the head teacher should consider any additional steps that they should take to ensure that their investigation and subsequent decision are fair. However, the final decision on whether to exclude is for the head teacher to make, rather than the police.[91]

Safeguarding, including guidance concerning pupils who have abused or sexually abused another pupil (commonly known as child-on-child abuse)

Schools have a statutory duty to make arrangements for safeguarding and to promote the welfare of their pupils. As part of this duty, schools are required to have regard to guidance issued by the Secretary of State for Education and must have regard to Keeping Children Safe in Education.[92]

---

91 *Exclusion from maintained schools, academies and pupil referral units in England*, DfE statutory guidance, September 2023, part fourteen

92 *Suspension and permanent exclusion from maintained schools, academies and pupil referral units in England, including pupil movement*, DfE statutory

Schools may receive allegations of abuse, sexual violence or harassment made by one pupil or pupils against another or others. This may well reach a criminal threshold and lead to behavioural sanctions.

Keeping Children Safe in Education contains essential detailed advice for governing bodies, proprietors, head teachers, principals, senior leadership teams and designated safeguarding leads about sexual violence or harassment in all schools. If a criminal investigation into sexual assault leads to a conviction or caution, the DfE advises schools to consider any suitable sanctions in light of their behaviour policy (if this has not already taken place), including consideration of permanent exclusion. If the perpetrator is not to be excluded, the school must in principle keep the victim and the perpetrator in separate classes. The question of the most appropriate way to manage potential contact between them on the school premises and/or on transport should be kept under continuous review. The nature of the conviction or caution, and the victim's views and wishes, will be particularly important in deciding how to proceed.[93]

When is permanent exclusion lawful?

Pupils may only be excluded for disciplinary reasons. They may not be excluded *because* they have SEN or are disabled, or because of any other protected characteristic; nor may they be excluded because of the behaviour of their parents; nor may they be excluded on the ground of their academic ability or attainment. The behaviour of a pupil outside school, however, can be considered legitimate grounds for an exclusion by the head teacher.[94]

---

guidance, August 2024, paras 23–26

93 '*Keeping Children Safe in Education*' (last updated May 2024) This sets out the legal duties one must follow to safeguard and promote the welfare of children and young people under the age of 18 in schools and colleges.

94 DfE exclusions guidance, August 2024, para 2 *R v London Borough of*

There will be occasions where a pupil commits such serious misconduct that a suspension is warranted to mark the seriousness of the pupil's misconduct. Permanent exclusion should only be used as a last resort.[95]

Two-part test for permanent exclusion

In England, a head teacher may only permanently exclude a pupil if both parts of the following two-part test are met:

- there has been a serious breach, or persistent breaches of the school's behaviour policy by the pupil; and
- allowing the pupil to remain in school would seriously harm the education or welfare of the pupil or others such as staff or pupils in the school.[96]

The use of "would" rather than "could" is deliberate. It is not enough that the pupil remaining in school "might" seriously harm the education or welfare of others in the school. The head teacher must assess the likelihood of repeat offending, and the impact that the pupil's return to school would have on others. A head teacher is entitled to have regard to the effect of a pupil's behaviour on staff, as well as pupils.[97]

Newham, ex parte X [1995] ELR 303

95 *Suspension and Permanent Exclusion from maintained schools, academies and pupil referral units in England, including pupil movement*, DfE statutory guidance, August 2024, page 3 and repeated throughout

96 Suspension and Permanent Exclusion from maintained schools, academies and pupil referral units in England, including pupil movement, DfE statutory guidance, August 2024, paragraph 11

97 *G v Independent Appeal Panel of London Borough of Bexley* [2009] EWCA Civ 785

> *Kieran has seriously breached the school's behavioural policy by selling ecstasy to younger pupils. Despite the drugs being found on him, and there being witness statements from numerous pupils detailing his sales and photographs of him in the act, he denies any responsibility. On reviewing all the evidence, and after taking advice from the police, the head teacher concludes that allowing him to remain in the school would seriously harm the welfare of others in the school.*

In Wales, a decision to exclude a learner should be taken only in response to serious breaches of the school's behaviour policy, and if allowing the learner to remain in school would seriously harm the education or welfare of the learner or others in the school. This means that first or one-off offences should only exceptionally lead to permanent exclusion in Wales.[98]

Relevant principles

A head teacher's decision under this test must be proportionate, reasonable, lawful, and procedurally fair (as must be any review and consequent decision by the board of governors, as well as the review and decision of any Independent Review Panel that is sought by the parents). These are classic principles of judicial review. For this reason, we look at, these principles again in Chapter 3 (review by governing board and Independent Review Panel) and Chapter 4 (judicial review).

98 These exceptional circumstances in Wales might include serious actual or threatened violence against another learner or member of staff, sexual abuse or assault, supplying an illegal drug or use or threatened use of an offensive weapon. See *R (on the application of LB, a minor, by her litigation friend SB) v Independent Appeal Panel of Newport City Council* [2017] EWHC 2216 (Admin), [2017] All ER (D) 57 (Sep): the appeal panel failed to make a clear finding that the pupil had used or threatened serious actual or threatened violence as set out in the Welsh guidance.

Proportionality

Proportionality operates in two ways. First, the sanction must be proportionate to the misconduct of the pupil. Second, proportionality requires the head teacher to balance the impact of the exclusion on the pupil against the harm that allowing the pupil to remain in school would do to the education or welfare of the pupil or others in the school. This will depend on the facts. Consider the following two scenarios:

> *Melissa is playing with a fidget spinner, forbidden in class under the behaviour policy, unless needed for a reasonable adjustment, at the back of the class. When the teacher tells her to bring the fidget spinner up and put it on the teacher's desk, Melissa obeys immediately and apologises. The teacher tells Melissa that she is recording a verbal reprimand and the confiscation of the fidget spinner but will give it back at the end of the day. Melissa has rarely been in trouble, and only for minor uniform infractions and occasional lateness.*

> *Jane is playing with a fidget spinner, forbidden in class under the behaviour policy, at the back of the class. When the teacher tells her to bring the fidget spinner up and put it on the teacher's desk, Jane refuses. When the teacher asks her again, she swears at him. The teacher calls for the Head of Year. When the Head of Year arrives, Jane puts the fidget spinner inside her trousers and tells him to get it himself if he wants it so badly. The Head of Year calls for the Deputy Head. When the Deputy Head comes into the room, Jane throws the fidget spinner at her, hitting her in the chest, and walks out. The class then ends, with only a fraction of the teacher's lesson plan completed. Jane has received several fixed-term exclusions for similar incidents that escalated following reprimands for minor infractions of school rules and a number of parents have reported complaints from their children at home about Jane's behaviour and the effect on their learning.*

It would plainly be disproportionate to permanently exclude Melissa. The incident involving Jane is more complicated. Although both incidents begin with the pupil playing with a forbidden toy, the first is easily contained. The second is not really about the fidget spinner; it is about Jane's oppositional behaviour and the consequences, which are the involvement of three teachers of increasing seniority and seriously disrupting a lesson. Whether the two-part test is satisfied in relation to Jane will depend upon a comprehensive review of the circumstances at play on the day and Jane's own circumstances – her behaviour log, any additional needs or vulnerabilities that she has, and so on.

The head teacher must assess the seriousness of the misconduct found to have occurred and look at all relevant factors arising from the available evidence. This includes any mitigating factors identified after an incident of misconduct. The head teacher must consider whether they have taken these and other factors that might have contributed to the pupil's behaviour sufficiently into account.[99]

> *Sylvia's mother has recently passed away from a long and painful illness, causing Sylvia to become withdrawn and angry at school. Sylvia is normally a very well-behaved pupil and does not have any exclusions on her record. When she is asked repeatedly to come inside from the playground, she snaps rudely and throws her book at her teacher, causing him to sustain a significant head injury. This is a serious incident, but it is out of character for Sylvia and she is very remorseful. The Head teacher assesses the situation, and speaks to her colleagues. She concludes that it is unlikely that Sylvia would cause any harm to the welfare of other pupils or staff going forward. She issues Sylvia with a one-day fixed-period exclusion, which is likely to be a proportionate approach.*

---

99 Suspension and Permanent Exclusion from maintained schools, academies and pupil referral units in England, including pupil movement, DfE statutory guidance, August 2024, paragraph 4 read with Part 4: Factors to consider before making a decision to exclude.

Reasonableness/irrationality

It is a fundamental principle of public law that decisions taken by public bodies should be reasonable, or rational. This generally means three things:

- The decision-maker (here the head teacher) should take into account all relevant matters arising from the information available to them.
- They should ignore all irrelevant matters.
- The decision that they reach should be one that could be taken by a reasonable decision-maker in the circumstances.

An unreasonable decision is one that no reasonable head teacher could have reached on the evidence before them.

> *A school allows Year 10/11 pupils to wear their own clothes. Two sisters, Diya and Amara, are known for wearing the same bright yellow jumpers every day without fail. One day, the girls' bathroom is found with obscene graffiti about the head teacher all over it. At the end of the day the Head Teacher reviews CCTV footage which shows two pupils wearing yellow jumpers leaving the bathroom around the time the graffiti is found. The video is grainy and only shows the back of the two pupils. The following day the Head Teacher proceeds to exclude Diya and Amara, assuming it must have been their graffiti. This is despite the fact that they were both off school the day before with laryngitis, having attended a protest that weekend. The admissions register and a note from their parent confirms this. Diya and Amara are in a position to argue that the Head Teacher's decision was not one that could have been reached by a reasonable head teacher on the evidence available.*

Lawfulness

The decision to exclude must be lawful. This means that it must be compliant with the rules and regulations relating directly to behaviour and exclusions as set out here and in Chapter 1. It must also be compliant with the school's wider duties to pupils, including those set out in the Equality Act 2010 (as to which see Chapter 6) and the European Convention on Human Rights.

As set out above, it is unlawful to exclude a pupil for a non-disciplinary reason.

> *Flora, who has chronic fatigue syndrome, requests to take fewer GCSEs than the normal school requirement, in order that she can properly manage at school. The head teacher does not accept that any pupil should take fewer than 11 GCSEs and permanently excludes Flora for this reason before she can enter Year 10. Not only is this likely to be a discriminatory exclusion but it is based on academic performance, which is not a disciplinary reason to exclude. This is likely to be an unlawful decision to exclude.*

> *Henry repeatedly disobeys academic instructions. This impacts on his grades, but it is for his persistent and wilful refusal to cooperate with his teachers that he is permanently excluded. So long as the school has done what it can do ascertain the cause of his refusal to obey instructions (including whether he has any underlying SEN) and has, if necessary, complied with their obligations under the Equality Act 2010 to make reasonable adjustments, Henry's poor attitude to work could be a lawful reason to exclude him.*

Off-rolling

Off-rolling refers, broadly, to the practice of removing pupils from the school roll in circumstances that do not fall within any of the fifteen grounds for de-registering a pupil that are prescribed in the Education (Pupil Registration) (England) Regulations 2006 (as amended in 2016 and 2023). Off-rolling tends to be an informal process. It can include asking pupils to leave a school because of their behaviour, their low academic attainment, or because a school cannot sufficiently address a pupil's SEN, causing a parent to have to home-school their child.

Any exclusion of a pupil, even for short periods, must be formally recorded. It would also be unlawful to exclude a pupil simply because they have SEN or a disability that the school feels it is unable to meet, or for a reason such as, academic attainment/ability; or the failure of a pupil to meet specific conditions before they are reinstated, such as to attend a reintegration meeting. If any of these unlawful exclusions are carried out and lead to the deletion of a pupil's name from the register, this is known as 'off-rolling'. An informal or unofficial exclusion, such as sending a pupil home 'to cool off', is unlawful when it does not follow the formal school exclusion process and regardless of whether it occurs with the agreement of parents. Parents cannot be pressurised into electively home-schooling their children.[100]

Research carried out by YouGov for Ofsted[101] suggests that the main reason for schools to off-roll a pupil is to manipulate league tables. It can be difficult to recognise, but signs of off-rolling practice at a school

---

100 *Suspension and permanent exclusion from maintained schools, academies and pupil referral units in England, including pupil movement*, DfE statutory guidance, August 2024, para 18–22

101 https://assets.publishing.service.gov.uk/government/uploads/system/uploads/attachment_data/file/800582/Ofsted_offrolling_report_YouGov_090519.pdf This survey looked at the views of 1,018 teaching professionals from primary and secondary schools across England.

include indicators such as exceptional levels of pupils leaving a school in years 10 and 11 rather than progressing to years 12 and 13. Off-rolling can also be difficult to prove; some parents would rather simply move than risk a permanent exclusion on their child's record, and may not be aware of their child's rights in this regard.

"Off-rolling" is currently defined by Ofsted as "*the practice of removing a pupil from the school roll without using a permanent exclusion, when the removal is primarily in the best interests of the school, rather than the best interests of the pupil. This includes pressuring a parent to remove their child from the school roll.*"[102] Looking for evidence of off-rolling now forms part of the inspection process, and is likely to result, the DfE guidance says, in an Inadequate judgment if there is evidence that pupils have been removed from the school roll without a formal permanent exclusion or by the school encouraging a parent to remove their child from the school, and leaders have taken insufficient action to address this.

Bilal is in year 9. He has had a series of behavioural issues this term. His Head of Year asks his teachers to record any incidents involving Bilal, for the purpose of a meeting with Bilal's parents. At that meeting, Bilal's parents are provided with a list of these incidents. They are also told to remove Bilal from the school by filling in a transfer form, or else he would be permanently excluded and end up at a PRU. Bilal's parents have not been educated in the U.K., and don't understand the transfer process or where Bilal will end up. They are told there is no time for questions, and they feel they must sign the transfer form at the meeting. The school has not given the parents adequate clarity and have put the parents under pressure to remove their child from the school.

102 https://educationinspection.blog.gov.uk/2019/05/10/what-is-off-rolling-and-how-does-ofsted-look-at-it-on-inspection/ – 10 May 2019

Human Rights

A decision to exclude must also be compliant with the pupil's human rights. The Human Rights Act 1998 came into force in the UK in October 2000. It incorporates the rights set out in the European Convention on Human Rights (ECHR) into domestic British law, which are the fundamental rights and freedoms of everyone in the UK, including pupils. Here we look at some of the Convention rights that may be raised in relation to the decision to permanently exclude. Some of these rights may be engaged by such a decision; others are likely not to be engaged. Human rights law is not always straightforward and parties may wish to take legal advice if a human rights issue is likely to arise in a particular case.

Right to education

The right to education is protected by Article 2 of Protocol 1 to the ECHR, which states that:

> *"No person shall be denied the right to education.*
>
> *In the exercise of any functions which it assumes in relation to education and teaching, the state shall respect the rights of parents to ensure such education and teaching in conformity with their own religious and philosophical convictions.*[103]

Although this Article is incorporated into national law by the Human Rights Act 1998, the United Kingdom has filed a reservation in respect of the Protocol 1 Article 2 which applies to domestic interpretation of

---

103 For an overview of the European Court of Human Right's approach to what constitutes education under Article 2, Protocol 1, see *Campbell and Cosans v United Kingdom* (1982) 4 EHRR 293 at paras 33, 40-1; *Leyla Sahin v Turkey* (2007) 44 EHRR 5, at paras 152, 154-5; *Timishev v Russia* (2007) 44 EHRR 37. For Northern Ireland, see *JR 17* [2010] UKSC 27 on appeal from: [2009] NICA 14.

the right as well as to this country's obligations under the Convention at international level. The reservation accepts the principle of education in conformity with parent's religious and philosophical convictions "only so far as it is compatible with the provision of efficient instruction and training, and the avoidance of unreasonable public expenditure."

A right to education does not entitle a child to an education at a particular school. The requirement in the Education (Pupil Registration) (England) Regulations 2006, regulation 8, only to delete a pupil's[104] name from a register on specified grounds also does not establish a right of a registered pupil to continue to be educated at that school.[105]

The decision of the European Court of Human Rights in *Ali v The United Kingdom 40385/06* [2011] ECHR 17 (11 January 2011)[106] illustrates that when deciding whether an exclusion is proportionate, a court will consider whether a fair balance was struck between the exclusion and the justification for the measure. In *Ali*, the exclusion of a student from a maintained school during the investigation of a criminal offence, and subsequent removal of the student from the school's roll, did not constitute a violation of the right to education under Article 2, Protocol 1. The Court recognised that schools are entitled to use disciplinary methods to ensure compliance with their own behavioural policies. Discussion of recent behaviour-based judicial reviews, including

---

104 *R (S) v Head Teacher of Claremont High School* [2001] EWHC Admin 513

105 See *R (on the application of LG) (Appellant) v Independent Appeal Panel for Tom Hood School (Respondent) & Secretary of State for the Department for Children, Schools and Families (Interested Party)* [2010] EWCA Civ 142 and *R (on the application of S (A Child)) v Brent LBC* (2002) EWCA Civ 693, (2002) ELR 556).

106 Preceded by *A v Head Teacher and Governors of Lord Grey School* [2006] 2 AC 363

(TTT) v Michaela Community Schools Trust [2024] (the Muslim prayer ban case) are set out in the Judicial Review chapter.

Uniform policies may be justified even where they appear to intersect with a pupil's right to manifest their religion under Article 9(1) of the Convention. In the case of *Begum,*[107] the House of Lords (as it then was) considered the position in relation to a mixed faith school whose uniform policy forbade Muslim girls from wearing the jilbab. Shalwar kameez was permitted. The school regarded its uniform policy as being in the best interests of the school and as contributing to social cohesion and harmony among the pupils. SB wore the shalwar kameez for her first two years at the school before deciding that her religious beliefs required her to wear the jilbab. She was refused permission to attend and directed to go home and return wearing a school uniform. This could potentially have amounted to a discriminatory or unlawful exclusion. SB refused to wear the school uniform and was effectively out of school for two years. She brought a claim for judicial review, arguing that her right to manifest her religion was being limited and her right to education under Article 2 violated. The House of Lords found that Article 9(1) was engaged because the jilbab was a sincere manifestation of SB's religious beliefs. However, SB and her parents had decided that she should attend a school that they had known prohibited the jilbab. There was no evidence that SB would not have been able to attend another school where the jilbab was permitted. Accordingly, there had been no interference with her Art 9(1) right. Nor had there been any infringement of her right to education under A2P1, since that article did not confer a right to attend a particular school, and SB had not been denied access to the general educational provision available from the system as a whole. Even if there had been, the court held that the uniform policy had a legitimate purpose (protecting the rights and freedoms of others), the school was entitled to conclude that the shalwar kameez was acceptable to mainstream Muslim

107 *R (SB) v Governors of Denbigh High School* [2006] UKHL 15, [2007] 1 AC 100

opinion, and allowing SB to wear the jilbab could have significant adverse repercussions for other pupils.

Right to a fair trial

Article 6 of the European Convention on Human Rights (the right to a fair trial) is sometimes invoked in challenges to exclusions, particularly where the conduct involved might be characterised as criminal conduct. Unfortunately, it has been found not to be engaged by hearings taking place in the context of the right to an education. In the case of *R (on the application of LG) v Tom Hood School*,[108] the allegation was that the pupil had a knife in his possession (and therefore amounted to alleging criminal conduct). It was argued on his behalf that Article 6 was engaged and the higher criminal standard of proof should have been applied, rather than the civil standard (balance of probabilities). The Court of Appeal held that Article 6 was not engaged by hearing before an appeal panel and that the application of the civil standard of proof was lawful.[109]

---

108 See *R (on the application of LG) (Mother and Litigation Friend of V) v The Independent Appeal Panel For Tom Hood School & The Board Of Governors of Tom Hood School and others* [2009] EWHC 369 (Admin) and *R v Richmond-Upon-Thames London Borough Council ex parte JC* (A Child) (2001) LGR 146;

109 The Joint Committee on Human Rights disagreed with this judgment in views expressed in 2010/11. Their views came shortly following the *Tom Hood* case and after the ECtHR had then decided the case of *Orsus v Croatia* (App.No. 15766/03) (16 March 2010) which held that Article 6 *did* apply to an education dispute relating to the discriminatory treatment of Roma Children who had been placed in segregated classes. The Joint Committee considered that if Article 6 applied in this case, then so should it in the context of exclusions. In their view, Article 6 is applicable to school exclusions and the independent review panel process breaches this right as it provides no opportunity to challenge factual findings and, without the power to reinstate, fails to give practical effect to the judgment of an independent tribunal.

Right to private and family life, home and correspondence

Article 8 of the ECHR protects the right of the individual to respect for their private and family life, their home and their correspondence:

> "*... there shall be no interference by a public authority with the exercise of this right except such as is in accordance with the law and is necessary in a democratic society in the interests of national security, public safety or the economic well-being of the country, for the prevention of disorder or crime, for the protection of health or morals, or for the protection of the rights and freedoms of others.*"

There is currently no authority to support the conclusion that there is an Article 8 right to attend a school, or not to be excluded from a particular school. In *A v Essex County Council,*[110] the claimant, A, alleged that he was adversely affected as a result of being excluded from school due to his propensity for violence and thereafter remained at home pending medical assessment. A had severe autism, epilepsy and learning difficulties. It took 19 months for the Respondent to make suitable alternative educational provision for him. He alleged breaches of Article 3, 8 and 14, and that the failure to provide a disabled child with an effective education constituted a breach of Article 2, Protocol 1 ECHR and therefore justified an award of damages. The Court of Appeal found that none of the Convention rights relied upon were engaged in A's particular circumstances.

Child's right to be heard

Article 12 of the United Nations Convention on the Rights of the Child (UNCRC) protects the child's right to be heard. In England, pupils under the age of 18 are unable to lodge an independent review themselves and must rely on their parents or guardians to do so. However, the only route of redress for breach of Article 12 rights is via Optional Protocol 3 (a communications procedure adopted by the UN in 2014). The United

110 [2008] EWCA Civ 364

Kingdom has not ratified Optional Protocol 3, and so children in the UK cannot complain under the UNCRC if their rights are breached.

Right not to be discriminated against in the enjoyment of Convention rights and freedoms

Finally, Article 14 ECHR protects the right not to be discriminated against in the enjoyment of the rights and freedoms set out in the Convention. This should not be confused with the more general domestic protection against discrimination which is afforded by the Equality Act 2010 (as to which see Chapter 6). Article 14 is not a free-standing right; it is always considered in conjunction with another Convention right, in the sense that a pupil would need to show that discrimination had affected their enjoyment of (not necessarily breached) one or more of their other Convention rights.[111]

---

[111] *C & C v The Governing Body of a School, The Secretary of State for Education (First Interested Party) and The National Autistic Society (Second Interested Party) (SEN)*: [2018] UKUT 269 (AAC) – This case arose from the fixed-period exclusion of L for physically aggressive behaviour at school. It was agreed that L had a recognised condition that was more likely to result in a tendency to physical abuse. Regulation 4(1) Equality Act 2010 (Disability) Regulations 2010 excludes a number of conditions from amounting to "impairments" for the purposes of section 6 of the Equality Act 2010, including a "tendency to physical abuse". Accordingly, the First-tier Tribunal found that L was not disabled within the meaning of the Equality Act and dismissed this aspect of his claim. The decision was appealed to the Upper Tribunal, which considered the compatibility of regulation 4(1)(c) with Article 14 ECHR (read in conjunction with Article 2 Protocol 1, the right to education). The Upper Tribunal held that the application of regulation 4(1)(c) to children such as L did not strike a fair balance between the rights of the individual and the interests of the community, and was therefore disproportionate.

Equality Act 2010

Finally, the decision to exclude must be non-discriminatory. This is explored further in Chapter 6.

Procedural fairness

The decision-making process in relation to exclusion must be impartial; it must be procedurally proper; it must not involve or constitute an abuse of power; and it must comply with the rules of natural justice. For example, bias could give rise to procedural impropriety. So could the appearance of bias. A head teacher may act unfairly if they refuse to allow the pupil to provide their version of events; if they refuse to admit evidence that may exonerate the pupil; if they don't provide reasons, or don't provide adequate reasons, that enable the pupil and their parents to understand why the decision to exclude has been taken;[112] or if they don't provide parents with sources of free and impartial information.

Christa's parents receive a letter from the head teacher of their daughter's school. This says that she has been permanently excluded for "bringing the school into disrepute". Her parents contact the school and ask for clarity. The person they speak to says that Christa "should know what she has done". Christa refuses to leave her bedroom to speak to her parents. The head teacher has failed to confirm the reasons, let alone any clear and understandable ones, for the exclusion. This is likely to be an unfair decision to exclude, as Christa and her parents are entitled to know the case against her and have the opportunity to put her case properly.

112 *R (K) v Governors of the W School and West Sussex CC* [2001] ELR 311 – the failure to provide witness evidence on which the decision was based to the applicant handicapped his defence

Having said this, procedural impropriety must be significant. If there is a technical breach of procedure that doesn't or wouldn't have affected the outcome, it is unlikely to be enough to result in the quashing of the decision on review.

The DfE's guidance states that the head teacher should give the pupil an opportunity to present their case before taking the decision to exclude.[113] Where relevant, the pupil should be given support to express their view, including through advocates such as parents or, if the pupil has one, a social worker. Whilst an exclusion may still be an appropriate sanction, the head teacher should also take account of any contributing factors identified after an incident of misbehaviour has occurred and consider paragraph 45 of the Behaviour in Schools guidance.

Cancellation of exclusions[114]

The head teacher can cancel any exclusion that has already begun (or one that has not yet begun), but this can only happen when the governing board has not yet met to consider whether the pupil should be reinstated. Reasons for cancellation must be provided. Parents and pupils over 18 should be offered the opportunity to discuss why the exclusion was cancelled without delay. The pupil must also be allowed back into the school from which they were excluded without delay. The DfE's guidance does not restrict the reasons why an exclusion should be cancelled. In our view this represents an opportunity for head teachers to change their minds.

---

113 Suspension and Permanent Exclusion from maintained schools, academies and pupil referral units in England, including pupil movement, DfE statutory guidance, August 2024, paragraph 4

114 *Suspension and permanent exclusion from maintained schools, academies and pupil referral units in England, including pupil movement*, DfE statutory guidance, August 2024, para 13

Potentially relevant factors in decisions to exclude

The relevant factors to be taken into account in deciding whether or not to exclude will always depend upon the facts of the case at hand. It is not possible to produce an exhaustive list of factors that will always be relevant, or factors that must never be taken into account. Part 4 of the statutory guidance provides several *specific* considerations for head teachers and principals prior to deciding whether or not to exclude and the right process to follow. This now explicitly includes a requirement to consider off-site direction and managed moves.

Here are some of the (more detailed) factors that we think head teachers should consider when making their decision:

- Has the behaviour policy been regularly/recently reviewed? Is it fit for purpose (see discussion on this point in Chapter 1)? Should it be obvious to parents and pupils that the conduct under consideration would constitute a serious breach of the behaviour policy that would potentially result in permanent exclusion?

- Has a thorough, fair investigation has been undertaken? Is the decision is being made on the basis of the evidence gathered or is it being made in the heat of the moment before proper considerations have been explored?

- Have all applicable policies (including the behaviour policy and any others that might be relevant) have been reviewed, and has the evidence obtained via investigation has been considered in light of those policies?

- Have the pupil's evidence and views been obtained, recorded and properly considered as part of the case?

- Have all potential mitigating circumstances (bereavement, illness, known difficulties with friends etc.) and partial defences, such as provocation or history of bullying/harassment, been considered?

- If the pupil has been persistently disruptive:
    - Have staff behaved in accordance with the behaviour policy and any reasonable adjustments agreed to it, e.g. when to impose a sanction, when to escalate, when to access internal and external support? If not, why not?
    - Are there any obvious underlying causes, such as disability, learning difficulties or problems at home or at school?
    - Are there any specific triggers, e.g. difficulties with a particular lesson or teacher or the time of day?
    - What early interventions have been put in place?
    - Has the school previously discussed the pupil's behaviour issues with parents?
    - Has there been appropriate wider consultation, e.g. involvement with other agencies such as specialist teaching agencies, CAMHS, commissioned services such as Educational Psychology, Speech and Language Therapy, Occupational therapy or via children's social care? If not, should there be a referral now?
    - Are there any initiatives aimed at pupils at risk of permanent exclusion offered by the local authority?
- Does the pupil have an EHC Plan? Is more or different special educational provision required? Should an emergency Annual Review be called?

- If the pupil does not have an EHC Plan but is receiving additional provision at school, is there additional special educational provision that would help? Does the local authority offer high needs funding that might assist? Alternatively, should the pupil have an EHC Needs Assessment?

- If the pupil does not currently receive additional help at school, is there evidence of unmet needs that should be investigated?

- Is there any other pastoral support that can be provided by the school, e.g. mentoring, buddying, key person, counselling?

- Is the child a child in need, a looked after child, or are there other known child protection issues? If so, has there been any discussion with their foster carers or social worker?

- Are there any alternatives to exclusion to be considered? These could include a lesser sanction, managed moves, directing off-site to improve behaviour, alternative dispute resolution methods such as restorative justice or mediation in appropriate cases, new interventions. If not, why not?

- Has the head teacher contacted the local authority to explain the situation and seek advice and assistance? Our view is that there should always be a discussion with the local authority to explore any further resources or alternatives before the decision to permanently exclude is taken, particularly if the head teacher thinks that a managed move may be appropriate but cannot identify an appropriate school to receive the student or if additional needs are a factor.

- Is there any discrimination or failure to make reasonable adjustments at play in the circumstances under consideration?

- Is the decision proportionate, rational, reasonable, lawful and procedurally fair?

- Are there any other relevant factors arising from the particular situation or the pupil's individual circumstances to be taken into account?

Alternatives to permanent exclusion

A head teacher can withdraw an exclusion up to the point that it is reviewed by the governing board (including, if the circumstances so dictate, as the governors are hearing evidence during the hearing). It is sensible for the head teacher to look again at alternatives to permanent exclusion at this stage, to ensure that nothing has been overlooked. Schools should work together with parents to consider such alternatives, where appropriate.

The Local Authority must be informed about an exclusion. A local authority will have an exclusions officer or similar person who will have responsibility for exclusions in that local authority area.[115] It is important for the head teacher to proactively seek the advice and support of the local authority to ensure that there are no alternatives of which the head teacher is unaware that might avoid the need for a permanent exclusion.

Here we discuss four potential alternatives to a permanent exclusion.

Directing off-site to improve behaviour

This is discussed in Chapter 1.

115 This is a list of local authorities with responsibility for education: http://schoolswebdirectory.co.uk/localauthorities.php

Alternative dispute resolution methods

These might include mediation or restorative justice. It is important to consider these strategies, particularly where there is a concern that the pupil will be unable to return to school due to concerns about the welfare of others. In some situations, alternative dispute resolution might be a highly effective means of resolving difficulties between peers, or between the excluded pupil and members of staff. In other situations, they may not be likely to be genuinely effective or in line with good safeguarding practice. But they should always be considered before a decision is made to permanently exclude.

Managed moves

A managed move is an arrangement whereby a pupil moves from one school to another on a trial basis. Typically, the head teacher has concluded that the pupil's misconduct was very serious and cannot remain in his or her school, but has identified mitigating factors and/or signs that the pupil would benefit from a fresh start in a new setting. Subject to the consent of the pupil's parents and the admission authority for the receiving school,[116] it may be agreed that the pupil should transfer from the transferring school to the receiving school. At the time that the first edition of this book was published, this would usually involve a trial period, during which pupil would remain on the roll of the transferring school whilst attending the receiving school. However, the DfE has since published managed moves guidance which suggests that the DfE considers a managed move to be a <u>permanent</u> move, and not a trial period.

Much negotiation and sharing of information about the pupil may take place before the receiving school decides whether or not it will accept the

[116] Managed moves to another school are permitted under section 29A of the Education Act 2002 and discussed in the DfE statutory guidance for exclusions, page 22.

pupil. Particular care should be taken when considering managed moves in respect of children with EHC Plans or with looked-after status.

The receiving school should make clear to the pupil and parents what its expectations are in terms of behaviour, and the circumstances in which the managed move may be terminated. There are usually also discussions about suitable support and intervention for the pupil and a plan should be drawn up and agreed, preferably in collaboration with parents.

Genuine consent of the pupil's parents is of vital importance to this process. Head teachers and local authorities must never forget that it is unlawful to use the threat of exclusion to influence parents to remove their child from the school.[117] For this reason, discussions around managed moves should be handled sensitively and collaboratively.

If by the end of the agreed trial period the pupil has successfully integrated into the receiving school without any issues, the pupil's name will be removed from the transferring school's roll and added to the roll of the receiving school. There is nothing in principle to stop the receiving school and transferring school from agreeing to extend the placement if the move has been partially successful but not without difficulties (although unlimited or indefinite rolling extensions may be susceptible to challenge by way of judicial review).

If, on the other hand, the managed move is terminated (for example, due to the child's failure to comply with expectations as to behaviour), the consequences will depend upon local policy and the view of those around the child as to why the placement failed. It is rare, although not completely unheard of in practice, for a pupil whose managed move failed during the trial period to be permitted to return to the transferring school. In many local authorities, although not all, the default position is that if the managed move fails, the child will not be permitted to return

---

117 *Suspension and permanent exclusion from maintained schools, academies and pupil referral units in England, including pupil movement*, DfE statutory guidance, August 2024, paragraph 21-22

to the transferring school and will be deemed to be permanently excluded. Since managed moves may fail for a variety of reasons that cannot necessarily be predicted, and which may not be the fault of the child, predetermining the issue in this way may seem unfair, and at odds with principles of public law; but again, this has yet to be tested in court.

Head teachers should always give consideration to whether a managed move might be possible, but whether or not they are varies widely from area to area. In some cases, the head teacher may simply feel that the conduct was so serious that a managed move is unworkable or not merited. In others the head teacher may feel that the difficulties that the pupil is experiencing are unlikely to be mitigated by a fresh start in a new mainstream setting. The head teacher may feel that they know local schools well enough to be confident that a managed move would not be possible in a particular case – for example because schools are full or because no other school is likely to take the pupil on a managed move basis. In some areas it may be possible to seek the local authority's assistance to transfer a pupil to a PRU on a managed move, on a temporary basis to avoid a permanent exclusion whilst the local authority finds an appropriate place for the pupil, for example in a special school, but this will depend upon how alternative provision is arranged in the area. Independent Review Panels and courts hearing discrimination claims are likely to ask if a managed move was considered, and to look carefully at the reasons why it was not; head teachers must be prepared to explain why they did not think that a managed move was appropriate or workable in a particular case.

The extent to which decisions in relation to managed moves can be challenged by parents and young people through legal action, and the appropriate mechanism for doing so, remains unclear. Managed moves currently take place via a mixture of local policy, head teacher discretion and negotiation. There is no statutory framework relating to managed moves, and only one decided case (which relates to managed moves but is of little assistance in terms of clarifying the law around them).[118] This means that the scope for challenging a refusal to seek a managed move by a head teacher, a refusal to accept a pupil on a managed move, or any shortcomings or discrimination in relation to education provided by the receiving school during the trial period of a managed move, is currently unclear. It is at least arguable that:

- Local policies and protocols on managed moves should be *Wednesbury* reasonable (see Chapter 4 on judicial review) and compliant with the Equality Act 2010, as should decisions made under them by schools;

- Adequate reasons should be provided to parents for a decision to terminate a managed move;

- Receiving schools will owe duties under the Equality Act 2010 to pupils in the provision of education even if the pupil is attending on a trial basis only and is not yet on the roll.

- The termination of the managed move by the receiving school will not constitute an unlawful exclusion because the child was never on the roll of the receiving school.

- A consequential permanent exclusion by the transferring school may amount to an unlawful exclusion, depending on the circumstance

However, none of these propositions has as yet been tested in court. Accordingly, any parent or young person considering a challenge to a decision about a managed move would be best advised to seek legal advice as to the best way forward – and as without delay, since limitation periods

118 *R (on the application of LB, a minor, by her litigation friend SB) v Independent Appeal Panel of Newport City Council* [2017] EWHC 2216 (Admin), [2017] All ER (D) 57 (Sep).

under the Equality Act 2010 and the judicial review jurisdiction are both very short and not easy to extend.

Giving notice of exclusion

The head teacher must take account of their legal duty of care when sending a pupil home following an exclusion, whether permanent or a suspension. The head teacher must also take reasonable steps without delay to notify the "relevant person", who may be the parent of the pupil, or the pupil himself if they are over 18 years old, the governing board, the local authority (or if applicable the home local authority) of the exclusion.

The notice given to the parent of a pupil must contain the following information:[119]

- the period of the exclusion and whether or not it is permanent,
- the reasons for the exclusion,
- the parents' right to make representations about the exclusion to the governing board, how representations should be made, how the pupil may be involved in this, and arrangements around any meeting where the governing board is legally required to consider the exclusion (as to which see Chapter 3).
- If the pupil is of compulsory school age, the notice should warn parents that they are under a duty not to allow their child to attend school or to be present in a public place at any time during school hours, and state the days upon which they must ensure this (without delay, and at the latest by the end of the afternoon

[119] Given under s 104 of the Education and Inspections Act 2006

session).[120] Penalty notices may be issued where parents allow their child to be present in a public place during school hours without reasonable justification during the first five days of a fixed period or permanent exclusion.

- If alternative provision is being provided, the start date, start and finish times, address and to whom the pupil should report on the first day should also be provided. If this cannot be provided by the end of the afternoon session, a subsequent notice may be issued with this information, without delay and not less than 48 hours before the alternative provision is due to start. If the head teacher fails to meet the deadline, they must still serve the notice; it is not invalid purely because it is delivered late. The only exception to this is where alternative provision is to be provided before the sixth day of a suspension or permanent exclusion, in which case the information can be provided with less than 48 hours' notice with parents' consent.

Notice must be in writing. Parents may now be given an exclusion notice electronically (such as by email or text message). Otherwise, written notification should be delivered directly to the parents; left at their usual or last-known home address; or posted to that address. Ideally, notification should be provided in person or by telephone in the first instance to allow for any initial questions or concerns. Information provided to parents must be clear and easily understood, including

---

120 Education and Inspections Act 2006, sections 103 to 105. Failing to comply with this duty, without reasonable justification, is technically an offence and proceedings can be instituted by a local authority. A person guilty of such an offence is liable on summary conviction to a fine not exceeding level 3 on the standard scale (up to £1,000). A Penalty Notice, rather than prosecution, may be issued by the Local Authority to offer the parent/s an opportunity to discharge liability for this offence by paying a penalty. For more information, see the DfE's '*School attendance parental responsibilities measures – statutory guidance for local authorities, school leaders, school staff, governing bodies and the police*' (January 2015)

translation where required. Where information is sent home with the pupil, the head teacher should consider sending a duplicate copy by an alternative method or confirming that the information has been received.

If the child is excluded for a further fixed period, or is subsequently permanently excluded, the head teacher must inform the parents without delay and must issue a new notice.

When notifying parents about an exclusion, the guidance also says that head teachers should draw attention to various relevant sources of free and impartial information, including a link to the statutory guidance itself. For a range of advice lines and other resources, please see the list at the back of this book.

Recording a permanent exclusion – the admission and attendance registers

Permanent exclusions must be formally recorded. The law requires all schools including independent schools to have an admission register and, with the exception of schools where all pupils are boarders, an attendance register. All pupils (regardless of their age) must be placed on both registers. The proprietor of a school who fails to comply with these regulations is guilty of an offence and can be fined.[121]

Schools must take the attendance register at the start of the first session of each school day and once during the second session. On each occasion, they must record whether every pupil is: *Present; Attending an approved educational activity (which includes alternative provision); Absent; or, Unable to attend due to exceptional circumstances.*[122] The school must

121 Education Act 1996, section 434(6)

122 Alternative provision means the provision of suitable full-time education to those who would not otherwise receive it, including education for excluded pupils by local authorities; education arranged by schools for

identify the correct code to use before entering it into the school's electronic register, or management information system used to download data to the School Census.

For school exclusions, schools must use Code E: *Excluded but no alternative provision made*. If no alternative provision is made for a pupil to continue their education whilst they are excluded but still on the admission register, they should be marked absent in the attendance register using Code E.

Alternative provision must be arranged for each excluded pupil from the sixth consecutive day of any fixed period or permanent exclusion.[123] Where alternative provision is made they should be marked using the appropriate attendance code (Code B: Present at an Approved Off-Site Educational Activity).[124]

The name of a pupil can lawfully be 'deleted' from the admission register on the grounds prescribed in regulation 9 of the Education (Pupil

---

pupils from day 6 of a fixed-period exclusion; and pupils being directed by schools to off-site provision to improve their behaviour.

123 The Education (Provision of Full-Time Education for Excluded Pupils) (England) (Amendment) Regulations 2014 (the 2014 Regulations) provide that a governing board's duty to arrange education from the sixth day of an exclusion is prompted by consecutive fixed-period exclusions totalling more than five days. (The Education (Provision of Full-Time Education for Excluded Pupils) (England) Regulations 2007 (SI 2007/1870) (2007 Regulations), as amended by the Education (Provision of Full-Time Education for Excluded Pupils) (England) (Amendment) Regulations 2014 (SI 2014/3216)

124 Education Act 2002, section 29A. The legal requirements and statutory guidance relating to the power to direct a child to off-site provision, which applies to maintained schools, are set out in guidance on alternative provision: https://www.gov.uk/government/publications/alternative-provision.

Registration) (England) Regulations 2023. Regulation 9(1)(p) – permanent exclusion – is one of several prescribed grounds.

The effect of a permanent exclusion is that a pupil will not be allowed to return to the school grounds, other than to attend a governing board review of the Head teacher's decision. The name of a permanently excluded pupil cannot be removed from the register until the review has completed. Where a pupil's name is removed from the school register and a discrimination claim is subsequently made, the First-tier Tribunal (Special Educational Needs and Disability) or County Court has the power to direct that the pupil should be reinstated.[125]

All schools (including academies and independent schools) must notify their local authority when they are about to remove a pupil's name from the school admission register under any of the grounds listed in the regulations. When notifying their local authority, school must provide and record details of the pupil's residence, the name of the person with whom they will reside, the date from which they will reside there, and the name of the destination school (where they can reasonably obtain this information). In the notification, the school must inform their local authority of the pupil's destination school and home address if the pupil is moving to a new school. The school must provide information to their local authority when registering new pupils within five days, including the pupil's address and previous school (where they can reasonably obtain this information).

Duty of local authority to arrange suitable full-time education for permanently excluded pupils of compulsory school age

We saw in Chapter 2 that where a pupil of compulsory school age is the subject of a fixed-period exclusion of more than five school days, the school must provide suitable full-time education from the sixth day of

[125] *Proprietor of Ashdown House School v (1) JKL (2) MNP* [2019] UKUT 259 (AAC), and see chapter 6.

exclusion onwards. Where a pupil of compulsory school age has been permanently excluded, the local authority for the pupil's area must arrange suitable full-time education for the pupil.[126]

The effect of exclusion

Where a pupil has been permanently excluded from two or more schools, a parent can still express a preference regarding subsequent school admission, but the requirement to comply with that preference is removed for a period of two years from the date on which the latest exclusion took place. This means that a pupil can often be disadvantaged when applying for another school place following permanent exclusion.

This exception does not apply to the following:

- pupils with statements of SEN or Education, Health and Care Plans;[127]
- pupils who were below compulsory school age when excluded;[128]
- pupils who were reinstated following a permanent exclusion; or[129]

---

126 *Suspension and permanent exclusion from maintained schools, academies and pupil referral units in England, including pupil movement*, DfE statutory guidance, August 2024, part 6, para 89-90

127 See School Standards and Framework Act 1998, section 98(7)

128 School Standards and Framework Act 1998, section 87(4)(c).

129 School Standards and Framework Act 1998, section 87(4)(a).

- pupils who would have been reinstated if it had been practicable to do so.[130]

Further reading

Head teachers, governing bodies, local authorities and Independent Review Panels must have regard to Department for Education (DfE) guidance issued under section 52.[131] The Guidance must be followed unless there is a good reason not to do so.[132] The relevant statutory guidance in England at present is the DfE publication, *Suspension and permanent exclusion from maintained schools, academies and pupil referral units in England, including pupil movement*, DfE statutory guidance, dated August 2024.

The guidance should not be taken as a complete or definitive statement of the law nor as a substitute for the relevant legislation.

Parents and/or pupils who are facing a decision to permanently exclude will find the statutory guidance useful in understanding what the duties of the head teacher, governors and Independent Review Panel are, and in navigating the statutory scheme for review of the head teacher's decision.

We also recommend that all parties involved in an exclusion read the DfE departmental advice *Behaviour and Discipline in Schools: Advice for*

---

130 School Standards and Framework Act 1998, section 87(4)(b).

131 Education Act 2002, section 52(4)(b)

132 The School Standards and Framework Act 1998, section 68 introduced the duty for head teachers, governing bodies, local authorities and appeal panels to *'have regard to any guidance given from time to time by the Secretary of State*". The High Court confirmed that statutory guidance is "*a highly material consideration*" for appeal (and review) panels (see *R v Northamptonshire CC ex p W* [1998] ELR 391, approved by the Court of Appeal in *R(X) v Y* LTL 1/9/2005, unreported).

headteachers and school staff, last updated in February 2024. Further information about behaviour and discipline can be found in Chapter 1.

Where the pupil at risk of exclusion has an EHC Plan, or has a disability or learning difficulty that means they are receiving additional help at school, all parties should read the SEND Code of Practice: 0 to 25 years– statutory guidance on the Children and Families Act 2014, produced by the DfE and available online. If there is a concern that a decision to permanently exclude may be tainted by discrimination, the EHRC's *Technical Advice for Schools*, available online, is likely to be of assistance; see also Chapter 6.

The support groups and charities listed in the Appendix to this work do in many cases publish useful advice and forums online.

The Education Act 2002 – section 51A

> ***Exclusion of pupils: England***
>
> *(1) The head teacher of a maintained school in England may exclude a pupil from the school for a fixed period or permanently.*
>
> *(2) The teacher in charge of a pupil referral unit in England may exclude a pupil from the unit for a fixed period or permanently.*
>
> *(3) Regulations must make provision—*
>
> *(a) requiring prescribed persons to be given prescribed information relating to any exclusion under subsection (1) or (2);*
>
> *(b) requiring the responsible body, in prescribed cases, to consider whether the pupil should be reinstated;*
>
> *(c) requiring the local authority to make arrangements enabling a prescribed person to apply to a review panel for a review, in any*

prescribed case, of a decision of the responsible body not to reinstate a pupil;

(d) about the constitution of a review panel;

(e) about the procedure to be followed on a review under paragraph (c).

(4) On an application by virtue of subsection (3)(c), the review panel may—

(a) uphold the decision of the responsible body,

(b) recommend that the responsible body reconsiders the matter, or

(c) if it considers that the decision of the responsible body was flawed when considered in the light of the principles applicable on an application for judicial review, quash the decision of the responsible body and direct the responsible body to reconsider the matter.

(5) Regulations may provide for the panel to have supplementary powers, and in particular may provide that the panel has the power to make a direction about the effect on an excluded pupil of a recommendation under subsection (4)(b) or a direction under subsection (4)(c).

(6) In a case where the panel gives a direction under subsection (4)(c) to the governing body of a maintained school, the panel may, in prescribed circumstances, order an adjustment of the school's budget share for a funding period.

(7) Regulations must make provision about—

(a) how the amount of the adjustment is to be determined;

(b) the effect of the adjustment on the budget shares of other maintained schools for the funding period.

(8) Regulations under this section may also make provision—

(a) for the payment by the local authority of allowances to members of the review panel;

(b) requiring a person or body exercising functions under subsection (1) or (2) or under the regulations to have regard to any guidance given from time to time by the Secretary of State;

(c) requiring local authorities to give prescribed information to the Secretary of State;

(d) in relation to any other matter relating to the exercise of the powers conferred by subsections (1) and (2).

CHAPTER THREE

THE STATUTORY SCHEME FOR REVIEW OF A PERMANENT EXCLUSION BY THE GOVERNING BOARD AND INDEPENDENT REVIEW PANEL

Introduction and overview

This chapter describes the process by which a decision to permanently exclude may be reviewed. The more limited process of review in relation to fixed-period exclusions is described in Chapter 1. There are three potential stages of review:

Stage 1: Internal review of the head teacher's decision to exclude by the school's governing board.[133]

Stage 2: Independent review. If the governing board upholds the head teacher's decision to exclude, the parents may then seek an independent review by the Independent Review Panel. As we will see, the Independent Review Panel can only quash the decision and require or recommend the governing board to reconsider the decision to exclude; unlike its statutory predecessor, the independent appeal panel, it cannot direct *reinstatement* of an excluded pupil. There is no statutory mechanism for review of the

---

133 As set out in the introduction, maintained schools have governing bodies; academy trusts have boards of trustees; and PRUs have management committees. In this book we use the term "governing board" to mean all three, in line with the DfE's guidance.

Independent Review Panel's decision, but it is sometimes possible to challenge an adverse decision through judicial review (see Chapter 4).

Stage 3: If the Independent Review Panel so orders, reconsideration of the decision to exclude by the governing board. Again, there is no statutory mechanism for review of the governing board's decision at this point, but it may be possible to challenge their decision via a claim for judicial review (see Chapter 4).

In this chapter we look at each of these stages.

The Governing Board's duties in relation to exclusions

All governing boards, no matter what type of school or how many schools they govern, have three core functions:

- Ensuring clarity of vision, ethos and strategic direction;
- Holding executive leaders to account for the educational performance of the organisation and its pupils, and the effective and efficient performance management of staff; and
- Overseeing the financial performance of the organisation and making sure its money is well spent.[134]

Governing boards, therefore, play a significant part in holding executive leaders to account for the lawful use of exclusion (including compliance with the Equality Act 2010). Governing boards must have regard to Department for Education (DfE) guidance issued under section 52 of the Education Act 2002. The relevant statutory guidance in England at

134 School Governance (Roles, Procedures and Allowances) (England) Regulations 2013 and the Academies Financial Handbook 2018; See also the DfE's 'Governance Handbook: for academies, multi-academy trusts and maintained schools (March 2019).

present has already been referred to at length in Chapter 2: it is the DfE publication, *Suspension and permanent exclusion from maintained schools, academies and pupil referral units in England, including pupil movement, DfE statutory guidance, August 2024*. Thus, the governing board has key legal responsibilities in relation to reviewing the head teacher's exclusion decisions.[135]

Governing bodies are allowed to delegate most of their functions, including disciplinary matters and review of exclusion, to committees. Accordingly, the governing board's[136] review of the decision to exclude may be carried out by a disciplinary subcommittee as long as it consists of at least 3 governors.[137]

Governing bodies of maintained schools also have a duty to make arrangements to ensure that their functions are carried out with a view to safeguarding and promoting the welfare of children.[138] The proprietors of Academies have a similar duty under paragraph 7 of Schedule 1 to the Education (Independent School Standards) (England) Regulations 2010. They must ensure that arrangements are made to safeguard and promote the welfare of pupils.

---

135 Education Act 2002, section 51A and The School Discipline (Pupil Exclusions and Reviews) (England) Regulations 2012.

136 School Governance (Roles, Procedures and Allowances) (England) Regulations 2013, regulation 18(1)(a)

137 School Governance (Roles, Procedures and Allowances) (England) Regulations 2013, regulation 22(3)

138 Education Act 2002, section175

Time limits for governing board review of permanent exclusions

The head teacher must inform the governing board of an exclusion without delay where the exclusion is permanent.[139]

The governing board must consider parents' representations about an exclusion. Where the exclusion is permanent, the governing board **must** consider whether or not to reinstate the pupil within 15 school days of receiving notice of the exclusion.[140] Where the exclusion would result in the pupil missing a public examination or national curriculum test, the governing board **must** consider reinstating the pupil before the date of the examination of the test (so far as reasonably practicable) and in any event within 15 school days of receiving notice of the exclusion.[141]

Giving notice of exclusion

As set out in Chapter 2, the head teacher must give notice in writing to the relevant person of the period of the exclusion and the reasons for it (that being the pupil's parent if they are under 18, or the pupil themselves if they are over 18). The notice must include information about how the parents or pupil can make representations about the decision to the governing board. This includes the means by which representations may be made and where and to whom representations should be sent. It should also state, where a meeting of the governing board is to consider the exclusion, that the relevant person may attend and be represented at

139 School Discipline (Pupil Exclusions and Reviews) Regulations 2012, regulation 5(2)–(3)

140 The School Discipline (Pupil Exclusions and Reviews) (England) Regulations 2012, regulation 5. If the pupil has been permanently excluded, this means the home authority of the pupil too.

141 The School Discipline (Pupil Exclusions and Reviews) (England) Regulations 2012, regulation 5.

the meeting (at their own expense)[142] and may be accompanied by a friend. It must also state that where the pupil is not the relevant person, the pupil may also be involved in the process of making representations, and set out how the pupil may be involved.[143]

Pupil's registration status pending review

During this period, the pupil remains on the school roll. Their name cannot lawfully be deleted until any review is determined, the time limit for applying for an Independent Review Panel has expired, and no application for review has been made. If an Independent Review has been applied for within that time, the pupil's name cannot be removed from the school's roll until that review has been determined or abandoned.[144]

As set out previously, governing bodies must arrange suitable full-time education for excluded pupils from the sixth school day of the exclusion for pupils of compulsory school age (except for Year 11 pupils who have no more public exams).[145]

The governing board's duty to review an exclusion

The Board must use reasonable endeavours to arrange a meeting for a date and time that is convenient to all parties. For permanent exclusions

142 Any expense in connection with the representation of the relevant person is treated as the expense of the relevant person, rather than the school or local authority.

143 The School Discipline (Pupil Exclusions and Reviews) (England) Regulations 2012, regulation 6

144 School Attendance (Pupil Registration) (England) Regulations 2023, regulation 5(d)–(e)

145 Education and Inspections Act 2006, section 100.

the meeting must take place within 15 school days[146] of receiving notice of a permanent exclusion.[147]

Power to adjourn a meeting of the governing board

There is no express power to enable the governing board to adjourn a meeting. However, the relevant regulations require the governing board to "take reasonable steps to arrange a meeting"[148] within the requisite time limit. This may give governors some flexibility if, for example, an adjournment is necessary to ensure a fair hearing. There is no set maximum or minimum duration for a meeting of the governing board.

Preparing for the meeting

Members of the governing board should not discuss the exclusion with any party outside the meeting. The governor disciplinary panel should not include members who have themselves taught the pupil being excluded.[149]

Any available written evidence, including witness statements and other relevant information, such as those relating to a pupil's SEN and the pupil's school record, should be provided by the governors in advance of the meeting, and should, if possible, be circulated (together with information about the hearing including a list of attendees) to all parties at least 5 school days in advance of the meeting). They must allow parents

---

146 School Discipline (Pupil Exclusions and Reviews) (England) Regulations 2012, regulation 6(7)(a)

147 *Suspension and permanent exclusion from maintained schools, academies and pupil referral units in England, including pupil movement*, DfE statutory guidance, August 2024, paragraph 100

148 School Discipline (Pupil Exclusions and Reviews) (England) Regulations 2012, regulation 6(3)(c)

149 *R v Board of Governors of Stoke Newington School, ex p M* (21 January 1992, unreported)

and the pupil (if attending) to be accompanied by a friend or representative. The governing board must consider whether attendees require reasonable adjustments under the Equality Act (as to which see Chapter 6).

Most importantly, the governing board must consider exactly how it will assist and support the excluded pupil to attend and to be heard at the meeting, and how to help the pupil provide their views.[150]

<u>Who must be invited to the meeting of the governing board?</u>

The following parties must be invited to a meeting of the governing board and allowed to make representations:

- parents (and, where requested, a representative or friend) or the pupil if they are over 18;
- the head teacher; and
- a representative of the local authority (in the case of a maintained school or PRU).
- The child's social worker, if the pupil has one
- The virtual school head (VSH) if the child is a looked after child (LAC)

Parents may request that the local authority and/or (if the pupil is being educated outside of their local authority's area) the home local authority attend a meeting of an academy's governing board as an observer; that

150 *Suspension and permanent exclusion from maintained schools, academies and pupil referral units in England, including pupil movement*, DfE statutory guidance, August 2024, para 4, 43, 112, 121.

representative may only make representations with the governing board's consent.

Encouraging the pupil to feed in

The governing board must enable and encourage the pupil to attend and be heard (and if the pupil has decided not to attend, to feed their views into the hearing) and proactively identify ways in which they can support the pupil to do this,[151] taking into account the pupil's age and understanding. It must be made clear to the parents and pupil in advance (most obviously by including the information in the invitation to the meeting) that the pupil is encouraged to attend, that the governing board will take into account the pupil's age and understanding, and that steps will be taken to assist the pupil to contribute at the meeting, for example by being allowed to bring a friend and by providing information accessible to them. For disabled pupils and parents, the governing board must consider appropriate reasonable adjustments that can be made to support their attendance and contribution.

If the parents and/or pupil do not wish the pupil to attend, the governing board should make it clear that the pupil can also make representations or give views in other ways, such as a written statement presented by their parents or by other means such as an audio or video statement played to the governors.

Parents may want to ask their child to provide an oral or written statement to the governors: this could include setting out their account of the incident or incidents leading to the decision to exclude; it might set out mitigating circumstances; it might simply be an apology and an expression of insight and remorse. Governing bodies should identify steps to ensure all parties will be supported to put their case and have their

151 *Suspension and permanent exclusion from maintained schools, academies and pupil referral units in England, including pupil movement*, DfE statutory guidance, August 2024, para 4, 43, 112, 121

views properly heard.[152] This will include compliance with its obligations under the Equality Act 2010.

Format of the governing board's meeting

There is no statutory format for a governing board meeting. Typically, however, meetings following the following structure:

1. Introductions
2. Head teacher statement
3. Panel and parent ask questions of the head teacher
4. Parent statement
5. The panel and head teacher ask questions of the parent (and pupil, if present)
6. The parties ask questions of the LA representative, the social worker and/or virtual school head, if attending
7. Head teacher closing statement
8. Parent closing statement

The governors should clearly set out the steps that they will take to ensure that all parties will be supported to participate and have their views heard (particularly in relation to pupils under 18 who wish to give evidence). Minutes must be taken (as to which see below). Before making its decision, the governing board should ask all parties to withdraw.

152 *Suspension and permanent exclusion from maintained schools, academies and pupil referral units in England, including pupil movement*, DfE statutory guidance, August 2024, para 112

The governing board will be assisted by a clerk. This must not be the head teacher. Frequently clerks are provided by the local authority; alternatively, a junior barrister or solicitor may be instructed to clerk, although there is no requirement for the clerk to be legally qualified. The clerk will take minutes and may also provide legal advice. The clerk is allowed to stay with the committee during its deliberations to help the governing board by referring to the notes, and to draft the decision letter. However, the clerk must not take part in the decision-making.

Fact-finding, evidence, and standard of proof

In the light of its consideration, the governing board can either:

- decline to reinstate the pupil; or
- direct reinstatement of the pupil immediately or on a particular date.[153]

In some cases there may be very little dispute about the facts giving rise to the exclusion. In other cases there may be considerable factual dispute. Where the head teacher's fact-finding is disputed, the governing board will be required to decide what the underlying facts in relation to an exclusion are. This means that the governing board may hear or read evidence and consider other documentary or real evidence (CCTV, audio recordings, Snapchat videos). It will be important for parents and/or their representatives to analyse the facts and available evidence carefully, and to consider how best to present their child's case to the governing board. On the one hand, parents must be alive to any potential issues with the evidence, such as obvious inconsistencies or improbabilities; obvious lines of investigation not followed up; evidence that should exist but has not appeared in the bundle; and inappropriate tactics such as aggressive,

153 *Suspension and permanent exclusion from maintained schools, academies and pupil referral units in England, including pupil movement*, DfE statutory guidance, August 2024, para 118

heavy-handed or highly-leading questions of their child or other witnesses. On the other hand, parents should also do their best to look objectively at their child's account against the background of the evidence elsewhere in the case; form a realistic and pragmatic view as to where the weight of the evidence is; and pitch their arguments accordingly.

It may be that further investigation is required. In *R v Camden London Borough and the Governors of the Hampstead School, ex p H*[154] a vulnerable child was injured by another pupil, and neither the injured pupil nor his parent were invited to attend the governors' meetings to consider the exclusion of the perpetrators. On appeal, the High Court found that further investigation could and should have been made before the governors' decision. So governors are not precluded from taking active steps to seek further or better evidence, if they are not satisfied by the case presented to them by either party. A prudent governing body may consider this essential prior to making their decision.

When establishing the facts, the governing board must apply the civil standard of proof (i.e. the balance of probabilities), in the same way as the head teacher did.

Failure to disclose prejudicial evidence to parents is also a breach of the requirement for fairness, and is liable to lead to the quashing of the governing board's decision.[155]

Both parties should be given the opportunity to take the governing board through their arguments. It is often helpful to have arguments presented in writing as well as orally, although overly legalistic submissions at the governors' stage (if the parent is legally represented) are not always met with enthusiasm, though should not be shut down. Preparing a list of

---

154 [1996] ELR 360, CA

155 See *R v Governors of Dunraven School, ex p B (a child)* [2000] ELR 156, CA, in which the school's failure to disclose a written statement made by another pupil was found to breach the rules of natural justice

issues or questions for the parties to go through at the hearing can also be helpful.

Procedural fairness at the governing board's meeting

The governors must be satisfied that the head teacher's decision was procedurally fair. Procedural fairness in the context of the head teacher's decision is addressed in Chapter 2. However, the governing board must also ensure that its own procedure is fair. This includes avoiding bias or the appearance of bias. For example, the governors reviewing the decision must not have discussed the exclusion with the head teacher in advance, nor may they discuss the exclusion with the head teacher during the hearing or their deliberations; for example, they must not ask the head teacher to remain behind after the parents have left so that they can deliberate. The head teacher must not be allowed to vote on whether the pupil should be reinstated. The governors must make sure that parents have been advised of their right to make representations at the hearing, and that they give the parents an opportunity to make representations before the hearing is concluded. The governing board must also ensure that it gives adequate reasons for its decision in the decision letter.[156]

Making the decision

Where the governing board is legally required to consider reinstating an excluded pupil, they must consider the interests and circumstances of the excluded pupil, including the circumstances in which the pupil was excluded, and have regard to the interests of other pupils and people

---

156 *Suspension and permanent exclusion from maintained schools, academies and pupil referral units in England, including pupil movement*, DfE statutory guidance, August 2024, para 182 "pupils are entitled to know the substance behind the reason for their permanent exclusion and the school should communicate this effectively with the pupil. Whilst carrying this out it is important to ensure that any reasonable adjustments are made and recognise that the pupil may have additional needs (e.g., speech, language and communication needs, cognition difficulties or EAL)."

working at the school, and any representations about the exclusion made to them by or on behalf of the pupil, the head teacher or the local authority. It is important for governors to understand that they are not merely approving the head teacher's decision.[157] They are making their own independent decision as to whether or not to reinstate the pupil or to decline to do so.

In reaching their decision, governors should have regard to the fact that the decision to exclude must be lawful (which includes compliance with the Equality Act 2010 and with the Human Rights Act 2006), reasonable and procedurally fair, taking account of the head teacher's legal duties and any evidence that was presented to the governing board in relation to the decision to exclude. We looked at those principles in detail in Chapter 2 in the context of the head teacher's decision, and they are examined again later in this chapter, in Chapter 4 (judicial review) and in Chapter 6 (discrimination). The governing board will of course be aware that its own decision must also be lawful, reasonable and procedurally fair in the eyes of the Independent Review Panel if the parents seek a review.

Part 4 of the DfE statutory guidance sets out a range of factors it expects schools to consider. Here are some key questions that it may be useful to consider (it may also be useful to refer to the list of factors for head teachers to consider in making the decision: see Chapter 2):

- What preventative measures to school exclusion, including alternative provision, off-site direction, outreach support and managed moves, have been considered?

- Has the head teacher investigated the incident(s) with all relevant parties in a sensitive and fair way?

---

157 School Discipline (Pupil Exclusions and Reviews) (England) Regulations 2012, regulation 6(3)(a) and (b)

- Did the head teacher take into account the factors that could have contributed to the pupil's behaviour, e.g. mitigating factors or partial defences such as a recent bereavement, provocation, history of harassment etc?

- Does the pupil have any SEN or other needs that might be relevant to his/her behaviour? Is further information or expert advice required to understand the reasons behind the behaviour and how this could be mitigated in the future?

- Has there been any further evidence since the decision to permanently exclude that could affect the decision?

- Is permanent exclusion a proportionate sanction, consistent with the school's behavioural policy?

- Has the governing board looked at all the evidence available, and is there any further evidence that it needs in order to be satisfied on the balance of probabilities that the facts that the head teacher found were more likely than not to have happened?[158]

- Has all the evidence been provided to the parents/pupil?

- Has the governing board been provided with a full picture of this pupil's behavioural record?

- In the case of a permanent exclusion, is there more than can be done to avoid a permanent exclusion?

- Are there any possible alternatives, e.g. directing the pupil off-site or a managed move?

---

158 See earlier discussion regarding the standard of proof in Chapter 2

- Has the head teacher contacted the local authority for advice and guidance as to what other options or assistance may be available?

Parents not seeking reinstatement

In some cases, parents will not be seeking reinstatement. They may have concluded, rightly or wrongly, that the relationship between their pupil or themselves and the school has broken down, or that the school is simply not the right setting for their child. It is important that the governing board appreciates that this does not render their decision academic. In these circumstances, they will have decided that their child should move to another school, but may still be very concerned about leaving a permanent exclusion unchallenged. Doing so may reduce the schools available to their child; they may also be concerned about the extent to which it may figure in future stages of their child's education. It may just simply be unfair. The governors must consider whether or not to reinstate the pupil by looking solely at the decision to exclude and without regard to whether the pupil will in fact return to school if reinstated.

Remote hearings

Parents (if the pupil is under 18) or excluded pupils (if they are aged 18 years or older) can request a meeting to be held via the use of remote access but this should not be a default option. Remote access means via electronic means such as a live video link. The default position is that hearings are in person, unless the parent has expressed a preference for a remote meeting or an in-person hearing is not practicable due to extraordinary events or circumstances (school closure due to floods, fire or infectious disease). If technological or internet issues prevent the meeting from being held fairly or transparently then the governors must arranged a face-to-face meeting without delay.[159]

---

159 *Suspension and permanent exclusion from maintained schools, academies and*

Remote hearings must be held fairly, transparently and accessibly, making sure everyone can be seen and heard properly. Muting just the family whilst allowing the Head teacher to talk freely or whisper to the Governing Board determining the decision would, for example, be grossly unfair. Social workers and VSHs are allowed to join remotely regardless of the format – this will make sense given their usually heavy caseload and difficulty attending a meeting in person at short notice. If a governing board or arranging authority is not satisfied that a meeting can be held fairly and transparently via remote access, they should consult with the parent to discuss how a face-to-face meeting can be arranged that will be convenient for them.[160] [161]

Minutes

The governing board should ensure that clear minutes are taken of the meeting as a record of the evidence that was considered by the governing board. These minutes should be made available to all parties on request and be accurate. Article 5(1)(d) of the General Data Protection Regulation (GDPR) requires that personal data must be *"accurate and, where necessary, kept up to date; every reasonable step must be taken to ensure that personal data that are inaccurate, having regard to the purposes for which they are processed, are erased or rectified without delay*". The minutes constitute personal data and are subject to this requirement.

pupil referral units in England, including pupil movement, DfE statutory guidance, August 2024, para 242–253

160 *Suspension and permanent exclusion from maintained schools, academies and pupil referral units in England, including pupil movement*, DfE statutory guidance, August 2024, para 242–253

161 *Suspension and permanent exclusion from maintained schools, academies and pupil referral units in England, including pupil movement*, DfE statutory guidance, August 2024, para 250

Decision letters

If the governing board is legally required to consider reinstating an excluded pupil, it must notify parents, the head teacher and the local authority of its decision, and the reasons for it, in writing. Whilst there is no requirement to provide a decision on the day, a decision must be communicated without delay.[162] Where the pupil resides in a different local authority area from the one in which the school is located, the governing board must also inform the pupil's 'home authority'.[163]

The letter may be drafted by the clerk in accordance with the governing board's decision. It must include:[164]

- The reasons for the decision, in sufficient detail to enable all parties to understand why the decision was made
- If the decision was to decline to reinstate the pupil, the fact that the exclusion is permanent
- Details of how to ask for the decision to be reviewed by an Independent Review Panel
- Details of how to ask for a SEN Expert to attend the Independent Review Panel, at no cost to parents
- Details of the parent's right to make a claim (within six months) under the Equality Act 2010 to the First-tier Tribunal (Special

162 School Discipline (Pupil Exclusions and Reviews) (England) Regulations 2012, regulation 6

163 *Suspension and permanent exclusion from maintained schools, academies and pupil referral units in England, including pupil movement*, DfE statutory guidance, August 2024, para 84

164 School Discipline (Pupil Exclusions and Reviews) (England) Regulations 2012, regulation 6(b)

Educational Needs and Disability) in the case of disability discrimination, or the County Court, in the case of other forms of discrimination.

Removing the pupil's name from the register[165]

The governing board must ensure that a pupil's name is removed from the school admissions register if 15 school days have passed since the parents were notified of the governing board's decision and they have not applied for an Independent Review Panel, or if the parents have stated in writing that they will not be applying for an Independent Review Panel.

If an application for an Independent Review Panel is requested within 15 school days,[166] then the pupil's name must remain on the register until the review has been determined or abandoned, and until the governing board has completed any reconsideration that the Independent Review Panel has either recommended or directed.

Any application for review by an Independent Review Panel made outside of the legal time frame must be rejected by the local authority/academy trust.[167]

165 School Attendance (Pupil Registration) (England) Regulations 2023

166 An email sent at 21:06 on a Friday was sufficient to 'make' an appeal by the end of the day, even if it was not read until the following Monday in *R (on the application of P) v Haringey London Borough Council* [2008] EWHC 2357 (Admin)

167 *Suspension and permanent exclusion from maintained schools, academies and pupil referral units in England, including pupil movement,* DfE statutory guidance, August 2024, para 152

The Independent Review Panel

If a governing board upholds a permanent exclusion, parents have the right to ask for a review of the decision by an Independent Review Panel. Parents may request an Independent Review Panel even if they did not make representations to, or attend, the meeting at which the governing board considered reinstating the pupil.

History of independent reviews of exclusion

Prior to 2012, governing board decisions were subject to appeal by an independent appeal panel. In 2012, independent appeal panels were replaced by independent review panels.[168] An Independent Review Panel reviews the governing board's decision not to reinstate a permanently excluded pupil. The Independent Review Panel is independent of the school or academy trust, and of the local authority. Unlike the previous appeal panels, an Independent Review Panel cannot direct or compel a governing board to reinstate an excluded pupil. The Independent Review Panel can only:

- uphold the exclusion decision of the governing board;
- recommend that the governing board reconsiders its decision; or
- if it considers the governing board's decision was flawed when considered in the light of the principles that apply on an application for judicial review, quash the governing board's decision and direct that it reconsiders the exclusion.

[168] With the coming into force of section 4 of the Education Act 2011 on 1 September 2012

Time limit for parents to seek an independent review by an Independent Review Panel

Parents must lodge their application for a review by an Independent Review Panel:

- within 15 school days of notice (in writing) being given to the parents by the governing board of their decision to uphold a permanent exclusion; or
- where an application has not been made within this time frame, within 15 school days of the final determination of a claim of discrimination under the Equality Act 2010 in relation to the exclusion.[169]

The local authority must, at its own expense:[170]

- Make arrangements for the review of the decision not to reinstate a pupil who has been permanently excluded, at an accessible venue for all parties
- If requested to do so, appoint for the purpose of that review, a SEN expert to provide impartial advice on how SEN may be relevant to the decision to exclude the pupil permanently. The SEN expert's role is set out in paragraphs 232 to 235 of the statutory guidance.

169 *Suspension and permanent exclusion from maintained schools, academies and pupil referral units in England, including pupil movement*, DfE statutory guidance, August 2024, paragraph 151

170 School Discipline (Pupil Exclusions and Reviews) (England) Regulations 2012, regulation 7

Where parents' case includes allegations of discrimination

In Chapter 6 we look at the Equality Act 2010, and briefly summarise the way in which claims for discrimination under the Equality Act 2010 can be brought before the First-tier Tribunal and the County Court. It is important to bear in mind, though, that if a decision to permanently exclude is tainted by discrimination, the Independent Review Panel can take that into account in deciding whether or not the exclusion was lawful. Parents who have asked for a review of an exclusion that they believe is discriminatory may find Chapter 6 useful in preparing for the hearing before the Independent Review Panel.

Parents and/or pupils may be uncertain as to how best to approach a claim for discrimination: should the argument be run before the Independent Review Panel or should it be brought as a separate claim? The answer is that both are permitted:

- Parents have 6 months from any discriminatory act or omission to bring a claim under the Equality Act 2010 (see Chapter 6; it is important to look at the rules on time limits carefully, as they can be convoluted, and to seek legal advice if the position appears unclear).

- The fact that parents wish to bring a claim under the Equality Act 2010 does not prevent them from also seeking a review of the exclusion by the Independent Review Panel within 15 school days of the governors' notice of refusal to reinstate. In addition, if parents did not ask for a review by the Independent Review Panel within 15 days of notice of the governing board's decision, but subsequently bring a claim for discrimination under the Equality Act 2010, they can ask for a review by the Independent Review Panel after the Equality Act claim has been dealt with (as set out above). They cannot, however, seek a second review by the Independent Review Panel after the determination of the Equality Act claim, if one has already been held.

- The fact that parents have made, or intend to make, a claim of discrimination in relation to the exclusion to the First-tier Tribunal or the County Court, does not permit the local authority/academy trust to delay or postpone arranging an Independent Review Panel hearing.[171] Nor, importantly, does it prevent the Independent Review Panel from considering issues of discrimination in reaching its decision. The First-tier Tribunal, however, does not generally expedite disability discrimination hearings unless an IRP has already made its decision, given that the IRP decision could have the (desired) effect of the child's exclusion decision being reversed by the Governors.

<u>Constitution of Independent Review Panels and clerking arrangements</u>[172]

A review panel must consist of 3 or 5 members and a Chair. A 3 member Independent Review Panel must consist of a lay member to chair (this should be someone who has not previously worked in any school in a paid capacity), a current or former school governor who has served as a governor for at least 12 consecutive months in the past 5 years and who has not been a teacher or a head teacher during that time, and a head teacher/person who has been a head teacher within the last 5 years. A 5-member panel must be constituted with a lay chair, 2 school governors and 2 heads or former heads.[173] They must be independent of the local

171 *Suspension and permanent exclusion from maintained schools, academies and pupil referral units in England, including pupil movement*, DfE statutory guidance, August 2024, paragraph 153

172 School Discipline (Pupil Exclusions and Reviews) (England) Regulations 2012, Schedule 1

173 *Suspension and permanent exclusion from maintained schools, academies and pupil referral units in England, including pupil movement*, DfE statutory guidance, August 2024, para 161

authority and governing board of the school and be suitably trained. [174]

The independent review should be conducted in an accessible, unthreatening and non-adversarial manner.[175]

The Independent Review Panel may be assisted by a clerk to advise it, as prescribed, on procedure, law and statutory guidance on exclusions.[176] The clerk must be trained and have an up to date understanding of developments in case law which are relevant to exclusion. If there is no clerk, the local authority or academy trust must organise the hearing, circulate relevant papers and write the minutes. It goes without saying that the clerk must not previously have served as clerk to the governing board in which the decision was made not to reinstate the pupil.

The Independent Review Panel stage can be an opportunity to 'cure' any unfairness that occurred during a hearing before the governing board.[177]

Preparing for the hearing: the clerk and the parties

Just as the head teacher and governing board may need to decide what happened before deciding whether or not to exclude (or not to reinstate),

---

174 *Suspension and permanent exclusion from maintained schools, academies and pupil referral units in England, including pupil movement*, DfE statutory guidance, August 2024, para 162

175 *Suspension and permanent exclusion from maintained schools, academies and pupil referral units in England, including pupil movement*, DfE statutory guidance, August 2024, para 219

176 School Discipline (Pupil Exclusions and Reviews) (England) Regulations 2012, Schedule 1, paragraph 4.

177 *R (on the application of 'DR') v Head teacher of St George's Catholic School (1) Governing Body of St George's Catholic School (2) Independent Appeal Panel of Westminster City Council (3)R (on the application of 'AM') v Governing Body of Kingsmead School (1) Independent Appeal Panel of London Borough of Enfield (2)* [2002] EWCA Civ 1822

the Independent Review Panel may be required to decide areas of factual dispute. The clerk to the Independent Review Panel should ensure that thorough preparations are made for the hearing, particularly in regard to the following:[178]

- Finding out, in advance of the hearing, whether the pupil will be attending. If so, the clerk must consider what steps should be taken to support the pupil in participating; if not, the clerk must make it clear to parents/the pupil that they may submit a written statement or provide their views through a representative.[179]
- The clerk should inform the parents that they may be supported at the hearing by a friend.[180]
- In a case where there is an alleged victim, the clerk should try to find out whether they also wish to be given a voice at the hearing, and if so, consider how this should be achieved.[181]
- Normally it will be appropriate to rely upon written statements of witnesses who are also pupils rather than hearing live evidence. Pupils may appear as witnesses if they are willing to do so and if they have the consent of their parents (or are 18). If they do

---

178 *Suspension and permanent exclusion from maintained schools, academies and pupil referral units in England, including pupil movement,* DfE statutory guidance, August 2024, para 175–187

179 *Suspension and permanent exclusion from maintained schools, academies and pupil referral units in England, including pupil movement,* DfE statutory guidance, August 2024, para 176

180 *Suspension and permanent exclusion from maintained schools, academies and pupil referral units in England, including pupil movement,* DfE statutory guidance, August 2024, para 177

181 *Suspension and permanent exclusion from maintained schools, academies and pupil referral units in England, including pupil movement,* DfE statutory guidance, August 2024, para 178

attend, the clerk should ensure that their parents are invited to attend in support.[182]

- All written statements should be signed and dated, unless there is a good reason to anonymise them. If a statement is anonymised, it should be labelled so that it is distinguishable from other statements. Excluded pupils are entitled to know the substance behind the reason for their exclusion.[183]

- Character witnesses should normally be allowed (with the panel's consent) unless there Is good reason to refuse.[184]

- Parties are entitled to be represented, and their representatives may make written or oral submissions to the Independent Review Panel. Since space can be limited at these hearings, if a party wishes to bring more than one friend or representative the clerk should seek the panel's agreement in advance. Note that all parents may attend, and each may make representations and be represented.[185]

- The clerk should ask the school for evidence in advance of the hearing so that it can be circulated to the parties, including

---

182 *Suspension and permanent exclusion from maintained schools, academies and pupil referral units in England, including pupil movement*, DfE statutory guidance, August 2024, para 179

183 *Suspension and permanent exclusion from maintained schools, academies and pupil referral units in England, including pupil movement*, DfE statutory guidance, August 2024, para 181–182

184 *Suspension and permanent exclusion from maintained schools, academies and pupil referral units in England, including pupil movement*, DfE statutory guidance, August 2024, para 180

185 *Suspension and permanent exclusion from maintained schools, academies and pupil referral units in England, including pupil movement*, DfE statutory guidance, August 2024, para 183

policies and other relevant documents as well as witness statements that the governing board would reasonably have expected to take account of in reaching its decision on reinstatement.[186]

- Where the school's case rests substantially on physical evidence, and there is a dispute as to fact, the physical evidence should be retained and made available to the panel. If it is not possible to retain the physical evidence, copies, photographs or signed witness statements should be used instead.[187]

- Where the head teacher who made the decision to exclude has left the school, and has not been called by the school as a witness, the panel may use its discretion in deciding whether or not to invite them to make representations.[188]

- Finally, the clerk should inform the panel if there is any difficulty in obtaining requested documents. The panel can then decide whether the hearing should be adjourned so that the documents or material can be made available.[189]

---

186 *Suspension and permanent exclusion from maintained schools, academies and pupil referral units in England, including pupil movement*, DfE statutory guidance, August 2024, para 184

187 *Suspension and permanent exclusion from maintained schools, academies and pupil referral units in England, including pupil movement*, DfE statutory guidance, August 2024, para 185

188 *Suspension and permanent exclusion from maintained schools, academies and pupil referral units in England, including pupil movement*, DfE statutory guidance, August 2024, para 186

189 *Suspension and permanent exclusion from maintained schools, academies and pupil referral units in England, including pupil movement*, DfE statutory guidance, August 2024, para 187

Parents and their representatives may wish to provide written representations to the Independent Review Panel in advance, to be included with the rest of the papers when circulated. This is not essential, but parents may feel reassured if their submissions are read alongside what can sometimes feel like a very school-leaning bundle of papers.

If the case involves a technical point of law (for example, a discrimination or human rights argument, or unusual point in relation to judicial review) it is useful for both sides to provide written submissions to the clerk in advance, with relevant authorities (ideally no more than 2-3), so that they are in a position to advise the Independent Review Panel if required.

Parties may make notes and bring them into the hearing. Parents who are representing themselves may wish to think about the questions that they want to ask each witness or speaker in advance, and bring a note of the questions in.

This is a good point at which to remind parents to make sure that they are asking question, of school witnesses, rather than making comments to them, when it is your turn to question them. At this stage, ensure you frame each point as a question. The opportunity to summarise your case will come at the end. However sensitive the Independent Review Panel is, such hearings are inevitably particularly difficult for parents and it can be easy to forget relevant questions in the heat of the moment.

New evidence

New evidence may be presented to the panel even if it was not before the governing board. However, the school may not introduce new reasons for the exclusion or for the decision not to reinstate the pupil and the panel must disregard any new reasons that are introduced.[190]

190 *Suspension and permanent exclusion from maintained schools, academies and pupil referral units in England, including pupil movement,* DfE statutory guidance, August 2024, para 207

Evidence of which the governing board could not reasonably be expected to be aware cannot be taken into account in deciding whether to quash the governing body's decision, but it may be a relevant factor in deciding whether to recommend reconsideration of the decision to exclude: see below. The question will be whether[191] *if* the governors were acting reasonably would this evidence have been available to them (for instance, evidence they should have asked the Head teacher for, or evidence from the family that had been unreasonably excluded from the hearing).

<u>Standard of proof</u>

The Independent Review Panel must also apply the civil standard of proof (i.e. the balance of probabilities). This means that the panel should accept that something happened if it is more likely that it happened than that it did not happen.[192]

<u>Parents not seeking reinstatement</u>

The parents or pupil may tell the panel that reinstatement is not sought. This does not render the decision academic, for the reasons discussed earlier in the context of the governing board's review. This should not influence the panel's decision, just as it must not influence the governing board. The focus of the panel's decision is whether there are sufficient grounds for them to direct or recommend that the governing board reconsider its decision to uphold the exclusion.[193]

---

191 *Suspension and permanent exclusion from maintained schools, academies and pupil referral units in England, including pupil movement*, DfE statutory guidance, August 2024, para 208–209

192 *Suspension and permanent exclusion from maintained schools, academies and pupil referral units in England, including pupil movement*, DfE statutory guidance, August 2024, para 202; see also the discussion of standard of proof in Chapter 2.

193 *Suspension and permanent exclusion from maintained schools, academies and*

The SEN expert

The parent has a right to request the attendance of a SEN expert at the Independent Review Panel.[194] A SEN expert is akin to an expert witness, providing impartial and specialist advice to the Independent Review Panel about how SEN might be relevant to the exclusion.[195] They can be very helpful for cases where pupils have SEN/disabilities or who might have unmet/unknown needs that should have been better explored before the decision to exclude was taken.

Where present, the panel must seek and have regard to the SEN expert's view of how SEN might be relevant to the pupil's exclusion.[196] The SEN expert must themselves have regard to the statutory guidance.[197]

A pupil's SEN or disabilities should usually still be taken into account by the Independent Review Panel even without a SEN expert.

The SEN expert must be someone who has expertise and experience in special educational needs considered by the local authority/ academy trust as appropriate to perform the functions specified in the legislation.

pupil referral units in England, including pupil movement, DfE statutory guidance, August 2024, para 223, 225

194 The School Discipline (Pupil Exclusions and Reviews) (England) Regulations 2012, regulation 2, *Suspension and permanent exclusion from maintained schools, academies and pupil referral units in England, including pupil movement*, DfE statutory guidance, August 2024, para 189, paras 232–235

195 The School Discipline (Pupil Exclusions and Reviews) (England) Regulations 2012, regulation 16(1)(b)

196 *Suspension and permanent exclusion from maintained schools, academies and pupil referral units in England, including pupil movement*, DfE statutory guidance, August 2024, paragraph 210

197 The School Discipline (Pupil Exclusions and Reviews) (England) Regulations 2012, regulation 9(e)

They are expected to understand the legal requirements on schools concerning SEN and disability. Examples of suitable individuals includes educational psychologists, specialist SEN teachers, SENCos and behaviour support teachers. Recently retired individuals are not precluded from this role, so long as they can satisfy the local authority or academy trust that they have a good understanding of current practice and the legal requirements on schools in relation to SEN. Experience working in schools is also required.

The final decision on the appointment of the SEN expert is for the local authority or academy trust, but it should take reasonable steps to ensure parents have confidence in the impartiality and capability of the SEN expert. Offering a choice of experts may be appropriate.

Role of the social worker

Where a social worker is present, the Independent Review Panel must have regard to any representations made by them. This includes representations about the pupil's experiences, needs, safeguarding risks and/or welfare that may be relevant to the pupil's permanent exclusion. Where a VSH is present, the panel must have regard to any representation made by the social worker of how any of the child's background, education and safeguarding needs were considered by the head teacher in the lead up to the permanent exclusion or relevant to the pupil's permanent exclusion.[198]

Procedure at the Independent Review Panel hearing

There is no set format in law for an Independent Review Panel hearing. A typical format, however, is as follows:

198 *Suspension and permanent exclusion from maintained schools, academies and pupil referral units in England, including pupil movement*, DfE statutory guidance, August 2024, para 211–212

1. Introductions from the Independent Review Panel and attendees;
2. The school makes a statement;
3. The Independent Review Panel and parents ask questions of the school and any witnesses called by the school;
4. The parents make a statement;
5. The Independent Review Panel and school ask questions of the parents and any witnesses, called by the parents;
6. Questions are asked of the SEN expert and/or social workers and/or LA representative
7. The school makes a closing statement;
8. The parents make a closing statement.

Procedurally, witnesses should not be present before giving evidence, although the Independent Review Panel may permit them to stay after they have finished giving evidence.[199] No one, other than the clerk, should be with the panel in the absence of the other parties, including the SEN expert. Everyone apart from the clerk should be asked to leave before the panel deliberates.[200]

---

199 *Suspension and permanent exclusion from maintained schools, academies and pupil referral units in England, including pupil movement*, DfE statutory guidance, August 2024, para 221

200 *Suspension and permanent exclusion from maintained schools, academies and pupil referral units in England, including pupil movement*, DfE statutory guidance, August 2024, para 222

Making the decision

The Independent Review Panel reviews the governing board's decision in accordance with principles of public law which are already familiar we have already looked at them in the context of the head teacher's decision to exclude in Chapter 2, and the governing board's review earlier in this chapter.

- **Illegality** – did the governing board act outside the scope of its legal powers in deciding that the pupil should not be reinstated? Was the decision lawful in light of the law in relation to exclusion generally, the Equality Act 2010 and the Human Rights Act 1998?

- **Irrationality** – did the governing board rely on irrelevant points, fail to take account of all relevant points, or make a decision so unreasonable that no governing board acting reasonably in such circumstances could have made it?

- **Procedural impropriety** – was the governing board's consideration so procedurally unfair or flawed that justice was clearly not done?

For more detailed analysis of these grounds, see Chapter 4 (Judicial Review).

The guidance goes on to explain that procedural impropriety means not simply a breach of minor points of procedure but something more substantive, that has a significant impact on the quality of the decision-making process. This will be a judgement for the panel to make, but the following are examples of the types of things that could give rise to procedural impropriety: bias; failing to notify parents of their right to make representations; the governing board making a decision without having given parents an opportunity to make representations; failing to give reasons for a decision; or being a judge in your own cause (for example, if the head teacher who took the decision to exclude were also to vote on whether the pupil should be reinstated).[201]

As previously explained, the Independent Review Panel effectively carries out a mini judicial review of the governing board's decision; in carrying out this exercise, the Independent Review Panel can consider every judicial review ground, not just those listed in the statutory guidance.[202] Since it has to consider the interests and circumstances of the excluded pupil, including the circumstances in which the pupil was excluded,[203] the Independent Review Panel also inevitably looks at the original decision of the Head teacher.

Decisions need not be unanimous

The Independent Review Panel's decision does not have to be unanimous and can be decided by a majority vote. In the case of a tied vote, the chair has the casting vote.[204]

The Independent Review Panel's powers upon review

The Independent Review Panel cannot direct reinstatement of an excluded pupil[205]. It can uphold a decision; it can quash the decision and

---

201 *Suspension and permanent exclusion from maintained schools, academies and pupil referral units in England, including pupil movement*, DfE statutory guidance, August 2024, para 228

202 *R (CR) v Independent Review Panel for the London Borough of Lambeth* [2014] EWHC 2461

203 *Suspension and permanent exclusion from maintained schools, academies and pupil referral units in England, including pupil movement*, DfE statutory guidance, August 2024, para 114, 200

204 *Suspension and permanent exclusion from maintained schools, academies and pupil referral units in England, including pupil movement*, DfE statutory guidance, August 2024, para 204

205 As expressly provided by the Education Act 2002, section 51A(4).

direct the governors to consider reinstating; or it can recommend that the governors consider reinstating.

Upholding the decision

If the Independent Review Panel considers that the exclusion was lawful, rational, procedurally fair and proportionate, it can uphold the exclusion.

Quashing the decision and directing the governing board to consider reinstatement

The Independent Review Panel may only quash the decision if it considers that the decision was flawed when considered in the light of the principles applicable on an application for judicial review (i.e. illegality, unreasonableness, material procedural impropriety, discriminatory considered above and in Chapter 2).

In making this decision, the panel must only consider the evidence that was available to the governing board at the time that it made its decision. This includes evidence that the panel considers would have been available to the governing board, or should have been, and which it should have taken into account if it had been acting reasonably.[206]

Recommending reinstatement

Where the criteria for quashing a decision have not been met, the panel should consider whether it would be appropriate to recommend that a governing board reconsiders its decision not to reinstate the pupil. This should not be the default option but should be used where evidence or procedural flaws have been identified that do not meet the criteria for quashing the decision, but which the panel believe justify a

206 *Suspension and permanent exclusion from maintained schools, academies and pupil referral units in England, including pupil movement*, DfE statutory guidance, August 2024, para 208–209

reconsideration of the governing board's decision.[207] This could include when new evidence presented at the review hearing was not available to the governing board at the time of its decision. The Independent Review Panel may take this step where, for example, it has identified new evidence of which the governing board could not reasonably have been expected to be aware at the time of its decision.[208]

Limited financial sanction where reconsideration directed

Where the Independent Review Panel directs a governing board to reconsider reinstatement it may order a downward adjustment of £4,000 in that school's budget share[209] (in the case of a maintained school) or, in the case of an academy, order the proprietor to pay £4,000 to the local authority,[210] unless the governing board decides to reinstate the pupil[211] within 10 school days of receiving notice of the panel's decision.[212] The

---

207 *Suspension and permanent exclusion from maintained schools, academies and pupil referral units in England, including pupil movement*, DfE statutory guidance, August 2024, para 229

208 *Suspension and permanent exclusion from maintained schools, academies and pupil referral units in England, including pupil movement*, DfE statutory guidance, August 2024, para 229

209 School Discipline (Pupil Exclusions and Reviews) (England) Regulations 2012, regulation 7(5)(b).

210 School Discipline (Pupil Exclusions and Reviews) (England) Regulations 2012, regulation 25(5)(b); *Suspension and permanent exclusion from maintained schools, academies and pupil referral units in England, including pupil movement*, DfE statutory guidance, August 2024, para 260

211 In *Re L (a minor by his father and litigation friend) (Appellant)* [2003] UKHL 9 it was found that reinstatement back into the school after exclusion meant reinstatement back into the school, not necessarily back into any particular class or teaching arrangement; see also *O v Governing Body of Park View Academy* [2007] EWCA Civ 592

212 *Suspension and permanent exclusion from maintained schools, academies and*

Independent Review Panel cannot order a financial readjustment where it has only *recommended* a reconsideration.[213] Some will characterise this downward financial adjustment as a fine.

Communicating the decision

After the hearing, the Independent Review Panel must notify the parties of their decision and of the reasons for that decision without delay.[214] The Independent Review Panel has a duty to give reasons for its decision in its decision letter, and to be clear about the evidence upon which it relies to draw those conclusions.[215]

Challenging the decision of the Independent Review Panel

There is no statutory right of appeal from the decision of the Independent Review Panel. However, the Independent Review Panel's decisions may be challenged in the Administrative Court by way of judicial review. Judicial review is discussed in more detail in Chapter 4. In general, we would advise any party considering a challenge to the Independent Review Panel to seek legal advice and (in the case of parents) advice as to potential funding sources (such as Legal Aid) before proceeding.

---

pupil referral units in England, including pupil movement, DfE statutory guidance, August 2024, para 272–273

213 *Suspension and permanent exclusion from maintained schools, academies and pupil referral units in England, including pupil movement*, DfE statutory guidance, August 2024, para 260

214 School Discipline (Pupil Exclusions and Reviews) (England) Regulations 2012, schedule 1, para 19.

215 *R (on the application of T) v IAP for Devon County Council and the Governing Body of X College* [2007] EWHC 763 (Admin): The IAP's decision letter was inadequate and did not display a correct understanding of the law. Further, the panel had been wrong to say that there had been no evidence of discrimination, provocation or bullying. The case was remitted for a fresh hearing.

Minutes

The clerk must ensure that minutes of the proceedings are taken, including details of the attendance, the voting and the decision. The minutes are not public documents, but should be retained for a period of at least 5 years as they may need to be seen by a court of (in the case of a maintained school) by the Local Government and Social Care Ombudsman. The local authority/academy trust should be aware of its duties under the Freedom of Information Act 2000, the Data Protection Act 2018, and the General Data Protection Regulation (EU) 2016/679 as it forms part of UK law (the UK GDPR) when retaining information.[216]

The governors' duty to reconsider the exclusion following the Independent Review Panel decision

Duty to meet

When an IRP directs or recommends a pupil's reinstatement, the governing board has the opportunity to look at the pupil's reinstatement afresh. The governors must meet to reconsider the exclusion within 10 school days of the Independent Review Panel giving notice of their decision to either quash the exclusion or recommend reconsideration of it.[217]

---

216 *Suspension and permanent exclusion from maintained schools, academies and pupil referral units in England, including pupil movement*, DfE statutory guidance, August 2024, para 239

217 *Suspension and permanent exclusion from maintained schools, academies and pupil referral units in England, including pupil movement*, DfE statutory guidance, August 2024, para 258

Duty to reconsider conscientiously

Although Independent Review Panels only have the power to recommend rather than to direct reinstatement, it would still "*be a bold step for the governing board not to follow [an Independent Review Panel's] recommendation.*"[218] (R (CR) v Independent Review Panel of the London Borough of Lambeth [2014] EWHC 2461 (Admin)). Governors must conscientiously consider reconsider whether or not to reinstate the excluded pupil; whilst there is nothing to stop the governors from reaching the same decision as they reached previously, they may face challenge in the courts (e.g. by way of judicial review – see Chapter 4 – or as part of a discrimination claim – see Chapter 6) if they refuse to reinstate the pupil following the Independent Review Panel's recommendation, without strong justification for doing so.[219]

A Parent (on the application of) v Governing Body of XYZ School [2022] EWHC 1146 (Admin) provides further useful guidance as to the nature of the functions that a governing body must perform when undertaking a reconsideration following a recommendation or direction to do so from an IRP. It also shows that the difference between the IRPs powers to quash and direct a reconsideration, and to recommend a reconsideration, is a material one in law. It also demonstrates the high threshold that a claimant will need to pass in order to persuade a court to interfere with a governing body's decision on irrationality grounds. (See also R (RWU) v A Governing Body of A Academy [2024] EWHC 2828 (Admin)).

Accordingly, the governing board should be very mindful of the findings of the Independent Review Panel, including for example any question

218 Collins J, *R (CR) v Independent Review Panel for the London Borough of Lambeth* [2014] EWHC 2461 (Admin). See also A Parent (on the application of) v Borough of XYZ [2022] EWHC 1146 (Admin)

219 *Suspension and permanent exclusion from maintained schools, academies and pupil referral units in England, including pupil movement*, DfE statutory guidance, August 2024, para 259

marks over the evidence or the proportionality of the decision-making. The governing board is not prevented from taking into account other matters that it considers relevant. It should take care to ensure that any additional information does not make the decision unlawful. This could be the case, for example, where new evidence is presented, or information is considered that is irrelevant to the decision at hand.

The governing board should assume, in its reconsideration, that the pupil will return to the school if reinstated, regardless of anything said by the parents or pupil to the contrary. In our view this is arguably a slightly different consideration to at the first Governors' stage[220] and the IRP, where whether the pupil / the pupil's parent wants them to be reinstated is not relevant.

Requirements for hearing

There is no requirement that the reconsideration stage takes place as a formal hearing, with parents present. Parents may ask to attend, and some governing boards may agree, but there is no legal requirement to do so. There is no requirement in the guidance to notify parents of when this meeting will be. However, if parents know that a reconsideration meeting is taking place there is nothing to stop them from drafting representations to put before the governors during the meeting.[221]

If there are parties present at the meeting, they should be asked to withdraw before the decision is made, but a clerk may stay.[222]

---

220 *Suspension and permanent exclusion from maintained schools, academies and pupil referral units in England, including pupil movement*, DfE statutory guidance, August 2024, para 268

221 *Suspension and permanent exclusion from maintained schools, academies and pupil referral units in England, including pupil movement*, DfE statutory guidance, August 2024, para 264

222 *Suspension and permanent exclusion from maintained schools, academies and*

The governing board must ensure that proper minutes are taken of their reconsideration, and that they are made available to all parties upon request.[223]

Notification of decision and reasons

The governing board must provide the outcome of either a recommended or a directed reconsideration without delay to the parents, the head teacher, the local authority and, where relevant, the "home authority".[224] In its decision the governing board should demonstrate how the concerns raised by the Independent Review Panel have been addressed.[225]

The outcome of the governing board's consideration should be noted on the pupil's educational record, along with copies of any papers. If reinstatement is offered to the pupil and is turned down, the decision should be recorded on the pupil's educational record.[226]

---

pupil referral units in England, including pupil movement, DfE statutory guidance, August 2024, para 266

223 *Suspension and permanent exclusion from maintained schools, academies and pupil referral units in England, including pupil movement*, DfE statutory guidance, August 2024, para 265

224 *Suspension and permanent exclusion from maintained schools, academies and pupil referral units in England, including pupil movement*, DfE statutory guidance, August 2024, para 263

225 *Suspension and permanent exclusion from maintained schools, academies and pupil referral units in England, including pupil movement*, DfE statutory guidance, August 2024, para 259, para 268

226 *Suspension and permanent exclusion from maintained schools, academies and pupil referral units in England, including pupil movement*, DfE statutory guidance, August 2024, para 268

After reconsideration, if the exclusion is upheld, the school will be entitled to remove the pupil's name from the admissions register,[227] unless there is an ongoing claim for discrimination in the First-tier Tribunal or County Court. The decision of the governors – at this stage – to uphold the exclusion would be a decision capable of review, but this time only by way of judicial review.

Further routes of challenge

There is no further mechanism for statutory review by the Independent Review Panel in respect of the governors' reconsideration. The only potential avenues of challenge open to parents in the event that the governors refuse to reinstate, or to reconsider as recommended by the Independent Review Panel, are a claim for judicial review (as to which see Chapter 4) or, where the parents consider that the decision was tainted by discrimination, a claim under the Equality Act 2010 (see Chapter 6).

[227] Education (Pupil Registration) (England) Regulations 2023, Regulation 9

CHAPTER FOUR

JUDICIAL REVIEW AND EXCLUSIONS

Introduction and overview

Public bodies have a duty to act lawfully, reasonably and fairly; these principles, which were considered in Chapters 2 and 3, are the cornerstone of administrative law. Sometimes the decision-making of public bodies falls short of these principles, and there may be no, or no further, statutory or regulatory appeal against that decision. If that is the case, any person with sufficient interest in the decision ("standing" or "locus standi") can ask the Court to review the decision to determine whether or not it was made lawfully.

<u>Difference between statutory review jurisdiction and judicial review jurisdiction</u>

The DfE's statutory guidance only covers the statutory school exclusions review jurisdiction, i.e. from head teacher's decision to Independent Review Panel outcome and (if relevant) reconsideration following the Independent Review Panel's decision by the governing board. The judicial review jurisdiction exists outside that process. Whilst the jurisdiction includes the ability to scrutinise decision-making in relation to exclusions, it is far wider than that: judicial review has application across the spectrum of public action and decision-making, and has generated a huge amount of precedent and practice that is constantly evolving. It is a highly specialist area.

Although the principles that govern the Independent Review Panel's decision-making (legality, reasonableness, procedural fairness) are classic principles of judicial review, the statutory review process is flexible, relatively informal and presumes that the majority of parents and pupils will be representing themselves. Judicial review as a claim made in the Administrative Court of the High Court of Justice is highly formal and complex. It is governed by struct rules of procedure. Although litigants in person can and do bring claims for judicial review without legal representation, and although judges will assist them with procedure as far as is compatible with their duties of independence and impartiality, there is no doubt that bringing a claim for judicial review is much more complicated and stressful than seeking a review of a decision to exclude under the statutory scheme as set out in Chapters 2 and 3.

The importance of taking legal advice: complexity and costs consequences of judicial review

Vast and learned texts have been written on judicial review by some of the finest legal minds of the last 100 years. A comprehensive guide to judicial review is beyond the scope of this book. All that we can hope to do here is present a very broad summary of the main principles of judicial review, the outlines of the procedure, and some significant cases that have been decided in the context of school exclusions. The purpose of this chapter is to give readers an idea of the scope for challenge beyond an Independent Review Panel.[228]

In this chapter, and elsewhere in this book, we repeatedly stress the importance of taking legal advice as soon as possible after a decision that may be subject to challenge. We make no apology for this. Anyone contemplating a claim for judicial review must bear in mind the potential costs consequences of an unsuccessful claim, or a claim that is run inappropriately and results in the other side's costs being higher than they should be. In judicial review proceedings, the starting point is that the

[228] Many of the cases that are cited in this chapter refer to Independent Appeal Panels, the Independent Review Panel's pre-2012 predecessor. Independent Appeal Panels had a wider remit and more extensive powers including the power to direct reinstatement. The difference between the regimes should be borne in mind when considering a pre-2012 case.

unsuccessful party will pay the successful party's legal costs – even if the unsuccessful party is not represented themselves. The court has a discretion to depart from this starting point, and costs will only be awarded that have been reasonably incurred and are of a reasonable amount. However, given the potential risks and complexity, any reader contemplating a claim for judicial review is strongly advised to seek advice as to the merits of such a claim, including whether there are alternative remedies available, potential sources of funding including legal aid eligibility for themselves or their child, and likely costs risk if unsuccessful, before issuing a claim for judicial review

What sort of decision can be judicially reviewed?

The deceptively short and simple answer to this question is that the decisions of public bodies, and bodies that are exercising public law functions, are susceptible to judicial review. However, this is a very broad summary of a huge body of case law in which the public/private law divide has been examined at length. In this country, many organisations have both private and public functions, and many public functions have been delegated to private organisations. Where there is a dispute about whether a particular body is a public or private body, the court has to consider the functions of the body, and whether those functions have public law consequences. This is one of the reasons why we would advise anyone considering a judicial review claim to seek legal advice first.

Governing boards of maintained schools and academies, and Independent Review Panels

The provision of education by a state school or academy is a public function, and decisions in relation to exclusion by state schools, including academies, is likely to be susceptible to judicial review, provided that all other remedies have been exhausted.

Independent schools

The position is very different in relation to independent schools. The independent school owes duties to the parents in contract and separately to the pupil in tort. It is well established that such claims are governed by the terms of the contract for the provision of education, and not principles of public law. For this reason, judicial reviews of such decisions have generally failed. This means that whether or not an independent school is obliged to arrange an appeal hearing for an excluded pupil turns upon the terms of the contract, not principles of public law. [229] There is no remedy in public law against an independent school which does not follow the rules of natural justice.[230] The Court of Appeal has emphasised that whilst there may be a certain degree of symmetry between public law considerations of fairness and contractually implied obligations of fairness, the question ultimately is contractual: whether the parents "*has had a fair deal of the kind that he bargained for*" [231] . For further information relating to exclusion in the independent context, see Chapter 5.

Unlawful exclusions that are not permanent exclusions leading to review by an Independent Review Panel

The court will not review a decision where there is an alternative remedy: see below. Where the head teacher has issued a permanent exclusion, the correct route of redress is via the governors' review and then (if the result is unsatisfactory) the Independent Review Panel. However, there may be circumstances where an unlawful exclusion leaves a pupil in limbo. For example, an indefinite exclusion, or a conditional exclusion (see

229 *R v Incorporated Froebel Institute, ex p L* [1999] ELR 488, QBD; *M v W* [2006] EWHC 575 (QB)

230 *R v Headmaster of Fernhill Manor School, ex p Brown* (Times, June 5th, 1992): pupil excluded for bullying without an opportunity to respond to the allegations or appear before the head teacher or governors

231 *Russell Gray v Marlborough College* [2006] EWCA Civ 1262

Chapter 2) may leave a pupil in a situation where there is no lawful fixed-period exclusion, but also no permanent exclusion triggering a right of review by the Independent Review Panel. In these circumstances, if the governors refuse to intervene either of their own volition or once the school complaints procedure has been invoked, it may be possible to judicially review a head teacher's decision to do so, since there may be no other alternative. Again, in this situation we would strongly recommend obtaining legal advice as soon as possible.

Who can bring a claim for judicial review?

The general rule is that any person who has a sufficient interest in the subject matter of the claim ("standing" or "locus standi") can seek judicial review of it. Again, the question of what "sufficient interest" means has spawned a vast quantity of case law in which a number of relevant factors have been identified. A person who is directly and adversely affected by the decision that they seek to challenge is unlikely to lack sufficient standing. If there is a dispute as to whether a person has standing, it will usually be determined at the permission stage.

In the majority of cases relating to exclusion, which will relate to decisions by the Independent Review Panel or the governing board, the appropriate claimant is likely to be either the parent or the pupil; which one depends upon the nature of the claim and the circumstances.

The identity of the appropriate claimant may have ramifications for funding – for example, a child may be entitled to bring a claim in their own name and receive legal aid funding to do so, even where the parents would not be eligible. But great care must be taken with this, as the Court will take an exceptionally dim view of anything that looks like an attempt to manipulate the rules to secure funding that would not normally be available to the parent, by bringing a claim in the name of the pupil when the appropriate claimant was the parent.[232]

Parents and pupils contemplating claims in judicial review would be best advised to seek legal advice from a solicitor's firm with appropriate expertise as to whether funding is likely to be available and as to who is the appropriate claimant.

It would, in theory, be open to the pupil to bring a judicial review claim against the governing board, but this is unlikely to occur in practice. The JUSTICE working party identified only one case where this has happened.[233]

The grounds for a claim for judicial review

Limits of judicial review

It is important, at the outset, to understand the limits of a claim for judicial review. The court's function is to assess the quality of the decision-making, not (generally) to adjudicate on the merits of the underlying decision. The court will be reluctant to interfere with the decisions made by the decision-maker unless it is very clear that the process was substantially and materially flawed.[234] The court is unlikely

---

232 *R (B) v Head Teacher of Alperton Community School* [2001] ELR 359 (exclusion); *R (T) Hackney LBC* [1991] COD 454 (admissions); *R (JC) Richmond LBC* [2001] ELR 21

233 https://justice.org.uk/wp-content/uploads/2019/12/Challenging-School-Exclusions.pdf – see *R (on the application of CR) v Independent Review Panel of Lambeth U3C* [2014] EWHC 2461 (Admin). See also A Parent, R (On the Application Of) v Borough of XYZ [2022] EWHC 1146.

234 "*The general rule, when Parliament has entrusted a decision-making process to a specialist body, is that the courts will be reluctant to interfere with the decisions made by that body. It is operating in a field with which it (and not*

to provide a remedy where the flaws in the decision-making were minimal or technical and would not have made a difference to the outcome. Indeed, the court must refuse to grant relief if it appears to the court to be highly likely that the outcome for the applicant would not have been substantially different if the conduct complained of had not occurred, unless the court considers that a remedy is appropriate for reasons of exceptional public interest;[235] this is explored in the section of this chapter relating to remedies.

<u>Classic judicial review grounds</u>

For the purposes of this work, and particularly in relation to exclusions, there are three broad categories of ground upon which a claim for judicial review can be made, and a claim may be made on the basis of one, some or all of them. In addition, there is the principle of proportionality to consider, which can be said to be relevant both to the lawfulness of the decision and whether or not it is reasonable in the public law sense.

We have looked at these principles already in Chapter 2, in the context of the head teacher's decision to exclude, and in Chapter 3, in the context of review by governing boards and the Independent Review Panel. Again, this is a very broad-brush summary of a vast amount of case law which continues to evolve, and should not be taken as a comprehensive description of the specific grounds for challenge that may arise under each heading:

- The decision was unlawful (illegality). This could mean that the decision-maker applied the wrong law, exercised one of its powers in a way that it should not have done, or acted "ultra vires"

---

the courts) is familiar, and this is particularly the case where sensitive relationships are concerned.", per Brooke LJ in *R v Dunraven School ex parte B* [2000] ELR 165

235 Senior Courts Act 1981 section 31 as amended by the Criminal Justice and Courts Act 2015 section 84

(outside of its powers/capacity). In the context of the Independent Review Panel's decision-making, this might include misunderstanding the law that regulates the Independent Review Panel's jurisdiction, functions and decision-making powers; exceeding the powers given to the Independent Review Panel; unlawful delegation of the Independent Review Panel's powers (e.g. to the head teacher). Human Rights Act 1998 and Equality Act 2010 claims can also be conceptualised as a form of illegality[236] – however, as indicated above, the appropriate appeal route for claims involving disability discrimination, will usually be to the First-tier Tribunal, unless it involves a public law aspect of the Equality Act, such as a breach of the public sector equality duty (PSED), or discrimination interfering with a right under the Convention. Human rights considerations were considered in Chapter 2 and Equality Act claims are the subject of Chapter 6.

- The decision was unreasonable or irrational. This is the appropriate ground where the decision was so unreasonable that no reasonable decision maker faced with that set of facts could ever have come to it (often referred to as *Wednesbury* [237] unreasonableness). Alternatively, a decision may be unreasonable if the decision-maker failed to take relevant matters into account, or took into account factors that should have been discounted. Were the right questions asked, and sufficient enquiry undertaken to enable the decision-maker to exercise their discretionary power properly? Did the decision-maker take reasonable steps to ensure that it had the necessary information upon which to base a proper decision? It is important to

236 See *R v Devon County Council ex parte G* [1989] AC 573

237 After *Associated Provincial Picture Houses Ltd v Wednesbury Corporation* (1948) 1 KB 223

understand that *Wednesbury*[238] unreasonableness[239] is a range test: it recognises that in many situations there will be more than one decision that can lawfully and reasonably be made in a particular set of circumstances. Accordingly, the court cannot conclude that the decision was unreasonable simply because the judge personally would have made a different decision on those facts; it can only do so if it is satisfied that no reasonable decision-maker could have reached that conclusion. *Wednesbury* unreasonableness can be very difficult to establish and is usually relied upon along with other grounds.

- The decision is materially flawed by procedural unfairness. This may arise in a number of different ways, including where the decision-maker has failed to take an important procedural step (e.g. consulting, where a right to consultation arises); has demonstrated bias; has not given a party an opportunity to be heard; or has failed to give any or any sufficiently comprehensible reasons for its decision. In the exclusions context, examples of material procedural unfairness might include failing to allow the applicant adequate facilities to make their case; taking into account evidence or factors of which the applicant was not aware or without asking them to comment; failing to notify the applicant of the time and date of the hearing; allowing new reasons for exclusion to be introduced by the school at the Independent Review Panel hearing; denying an applicant access to reasonable documents; refusing legal representation; and so on. So far as reasons are concerned, it is well-established that

---

238 *Council of Civil Service Unions v Minister for the Civil Service* [1985] AC 374 HL, per Lord Diplock: a decision "*so outrageous in its defiance of logic or of accepted moral standards that no sensible person who had applied his mind to the question to be decided could have arrived at it*".

239 See *Secretary of State for Education and Science v Tameside Metropolitan Borough Council* [1977] AC 1014.

public bodies must give adequate reasons for a decision, particularly when the decision is particularly important.[240]

- The decision was disproportionate. Proportionality involves striking a balance between the general interests of the community and the legitimate aims of the state, and the protection of the individual's rights and interests. Assertions that public authorities have interfered with an applicant's human rights are typically met by defences based on justification, which have to be substantiated by evidence. In *R (S) v Brent LBC*[241], the Court of Appeal considered three consolidated judicial review appeals arising from school exclusion decisions. Although the appeals principally related to the lawfulness of the prevailing government guidance issued under the precursor to section 52 of the EIA 2006, the court proceeded to make a number of useful statements regarding the appropriate conduct of panel review hearings:

- the local authority must maintain an objective stance; it is not part of its function to press for a particular finding or outcome in respect of a pupil;[242]

- the panel must avoid permitting the local authority or any other party to unduly influence or monopolise the hearing through its representations;[243]

---

240 *R (Nash) v Chelsea College of Art and Design* [2001] EWHC 538 (Admin) per Stanley Burnton J

241 [2002] ELR 556.

242 *R (S) v Brent LBC* [2002] ELR 556 at [22]–[24].

243 [2002] ELR 556 at [25] approving the observations of Newman J in *R (T) v Head Teacher of Wembley High School and Others* [2001] ELR 359. See also *R (W) v Governors of Bacon's City Technology College* [1998] ELR 488 (failure of the chair to indicate the panel's need to hear from a pupil

- the panel must entertain any credible material, written or oral, which is reasonably and fairly capable of affecting what it has to decide[244]

- if there is a material conflict of evidence involving an adult witness, there is no reason why the witness cannot be invited to attend and be questioned. If a witness declines to come for no reason, or for an unacceptable one, the panel will be entitled to draw whatever inferences seem appropriate in the circumstances[245]

- the panel is entitled to restrict confrontational cross-examination of witnesses and to require questions to be put through or by the chair[246]

- whilst there may be good reasons for seeking to preserve the anonymity of witnesses, for example in the context of bullying allegations, use by the panel of anonymised statements has the potential to cause injustice. Use of such statements may be unfair; in particular, if they are damaging to the pupil in ways that he or she cannot be expected to address without knowing the maker.[247]

---

directly, as opposed to his loquacious representative, gave rise to unfairness).

244 [2002] ELR 556 at [27]. See also *R (W) v Governors of Bacon's City Technology College* [1998] ELR 488 (allowing a limited period of time for appeals was a dangerous policy as it would serve to unduly restrict the scope of inquiry and representations in some cases).

245 [2002] ELR 556 at [28].

246 [2002] ELR 556 at [28]. See also *R (W) v IAP for Bexley* [2008] ELR 301 per Burton J at [20]–[29] (it is for the IAP to hear all the evidence and consider any challenge to its reliability and weight).

247 [2002] ELR 556 at [27]. See also *R (B) v Head Teacher of Dunraven*

In *R (B) v Head Teacher of Dunraven School*[248] the Court of Appeal gave similarly useful guidance on disclosure in the context of exclusion hearings:

- if there are discrepancies within the material relied upon in support of the allegations made against the pupil, fairness will ordinarily dictate making sufficient disclosure to reveal such inconsistency[249]

- it is unfair for the panel to have access to damaging material to which the pupil has no access[250]

- disclosure of such material is not dependent upon a request by the pupil; the duty to ensure fairness is not conditional upon applications or demands more appropriate to adversarial litigation[251]

School [2000] ELR 156 (a governing board may, in some cases, be forced to elect to proceed in the absence of a statement or otherwise reinstate a pupil); *R (K) v Governors of the W School and West Sussex CC* [2001] ELR 311 (failure to provide witness evidence on which the decision was based to the applicant handicapped his defence) and *R (T) v Head Teacher of Elliott School* [2002] ELR 556 (decisions on admission are fact sensitive and the IAP, in each case, must be conscious of any possible unfairness).

248 [2000] ELR 156.

249 [2000] ELR 156 per Sedley LJ at [190]. Similarly, a head teacher with reason to doubt the reliability or impartially of a statement must draw such concerns to the attention of the IAP: *R (T) v Head Teacher of Elliott School* [2002] ELR 556 per Schiemann LJ at [37].

250 [2000] ELR 156 per Sedley LJ at 190.

251 [2000] ELR 156 per Sedley LJ at 193.

Time limits for bringing claims for judicial review

Judicial review is considered to be an emergency jurisdiction. Pursuant to CPR 54.5, the claim form must be filed (a) promptly; and (b) in any event, not later than 3 months after the grounds to make the claim first arose.[252] Unlike in other civil claims, the parties cannot extend the time limit for a judicial review claim by agreement or standstill, although such an agreement would be a relevant factor in the court's decision as to whether or not to extend time. The bottom line is that only the court can extend time to bring a claim for judicial review, and it has a wide discretion as to whether or not to do so in individual cases. Every effort must be made to bring a claim within time.

Matters are further complicated by the fact that the 3-month limit is a backstop limit; the core requirement is to bring the claim "promptly". This means that it is important to bring the claim promptly *within* the 3-month time limit. The claim could be time-barred if there is delay in making the claim within that time and the defendant acts to its detriment in the meantime (for example by committing to something that it would not have committed to if it had been aware that a claim in judicial review was likely).

Undue delay in bringing a claim can adversely affect the claimant in two ways.[253] The first is that at the "permission" stage (a preliminary consideration of the case by a judge of the Administrative Court to decide whether to allow the claim to proceed), the court may refuse permission to bring the claim at all. The second is that if permission is given, the court may nevertheless withhold relief (i.e. a remedy) at the substantive hearing (the final determination of the claim) if it considers that granting relief would be likely to cause substantial hardship to, or substantially

---

252 Although unlikely to be relevant to school exclusions, it should be noted that shorter time limits apply in respect of judicial reviews of some planning decisions and for some procurement decisions.

253 Senior Courts Act 1981, section 31(8)

prejudice the rights of, any person, or would be detrimental to good administration. Undue delay can preclude the grant of permission or relief in exclusion cases.[254]

Alternative remedies must usually be exhausted

Judicial review is a remedy of last resort. The statutory appeal route under section 51A Education Act 2002 must generally be exhausted before judicial review proceedings can be contemplated. The court may refuse permission to bring a claim for judicial review if there is an alternative means of redress available to the applicant, and where that alternative remedy would be effective.

For this reason, in terms of school exclusions, the statutory appeal route to the Independent Review Panel must, save in exceptional cases, be exhausted before judicial review proceedings can be contemplated.[255] This is the case even where the governing board hearing is flawed, because such flaws may yet be capable of cure through a fair Independent Review Panel hearing.[256]

---

254 For example, see *R (M) v Secretary of State for Home Department* [1999] Ed. CR 656.

255 *R (DR) v Head Teacher of St George's Catholic School* [2002] EWCA Civ 1822 [2003]; the legislation provided a full appeal procedure from the initial decision of the school's head teacher, first to the governors, and then to an independent appeal panel. See also *R (A) v Fernhill Manor School* [1994] ELR 67 and *R on the application of CR v Independent Review Panel of Lambeth* [2014] EWHC 2461 (Admin).

256 *R (AM) v Governing Body of Kingsmead School* [2003] LGR 371. The hearing before the governing board was very poorly conducted. The Head teacher had remained in the room whilst the governors deliberated. A number of documents were not made available to the appellant's father until the day before the hearing. The governing board had refused to

There have been a handful of exceptional cases in which permission was given to proceed with a claim for judicial review despite the claimant not having pursued their right to an independent panel or other mechanism for review. In one such case, compelling circumstances (severe mental health illness of the pupil and a substantial family bereavement) constituted compelling grounds for permitting the claim to proceed despite the existence of the statutory remedy.[257] In another case, leave was granted to apply for judicial review despite the availability of an appeal to the Secretary of State for Education under the provisions of the Education Act 1981 which then applied, although judicial review was refused at the substantive hearing.[258] Accordingly, where there are potentially alternative remedies that could be pursued, advice should be sought as early as possible as to whether judicial review is the right remedy, or whether another route should be taken.

The Pre-Action Protocol for Judicial Review

Prior to bringing a claim for judicial review, a claimant should "*generally*" comply with the Pre-Action Protocol for Judicial Review.[259] This is

---

allow the father to put in three exculpatory statements made by fellow pupils. The IAP, by contrast, was found to have gone into the matter with "*impressive thoroughness*" and its conduct of the appeal was found to be "*entirely unimpeachable*". This was held to have cured the defects in the Governing Body proceedings

257 *R (K) v Governors of the W School and West Sussex CC* [2001] ELR 311

258 *R v London Borough of Camden ex parte B* [1994] ELR 490

259 Failure to comply with the Pre-Action Protocol can affect prospects of recovering costs. See *R (Bahta v Secretary of State for the Home Department* [2011] EWCA Civ 895 at 59-71 and *R (Kemp) v Denbighshire Local Health Board* [2006] EWHC 18 181 (Admin). However, the Protocol is not appropriate where a claim would become out of time if followed. In such cases, the claim should be filed and the claim form used to explain why the Protocol was not used.

unless it is a '*very urgent case*', where a claim needs to be made immediately/out of hours (although even in a very urgent case efforts should be made to follow the pre-action protocol as far as possible, for example by alerting the defendant to the claim via phone or email if necessary, and providing them with a copy of the proposed claim even if it is in draft). This procedure is usually reserved for cases such as imminent removal from the UK in an immigration case. The Administrative Court usually takes the view that cases involving children who have been excluded or are currently without education should be expedited, and that is a matter to take into account when issuing the claim. However, the emergency/very urgent process should not be used unless there is a risk of exceptional and immediate prejudice to the child's interests if the application is not made immediately. Imminent important public examinations might present that sort of concern, but parents are strongly advised to seek legal advice before embarking upon an urgent claim that may not be warranted.

It is also important to be aware that commencing the pre-action protocol does not affect the time limits for starting the claim.

The pre-action protocol requires prospective claimants to send a letter to the Defendant body (in exclusion cases, usually the Independent Review Panel or governing board of the school) before making a claim. A standard form of this letter is set out in Annex A to the Protocol.

In cases involving school exclusions, it is likely that such a letter would contain the following:

- The date and details of the decision – most likely to be the date of the Independent Review Panel decision letter

- A summary of the facts and legal basis of the claim

- Details of the actions which the Claimant wants the Defendant to take (the remedy)[260]

- Whether, if the Claimant seeks further information, what that is and what relevance it has to the claim[261]

- Any proposals for alternative dispute resolution, such as mediation, discussion, negotiation, referral to any relevant ombudsman, etc. This is particularly important because the pre-action protocol specifically requires the parties to consider whether there is a form of alternative dispute resolution that would be more appropriate than court action.

- Any requests for pre-action disclosure. For example, in a judicial review to a decision to exclude it is reasonable for a claimant to seek disclosure of the minutes taken by the Independent Review Panel's clerk and/or those of any relevant governing board meeting. If the defendant refuses to disclose at the pre-action stage, an application for disclosure can be made to the Court in the event that permission is granted to proceed with a claim for judicial review.

- A proposed reply date, which is usually 14 days. This period may be shortened if there is any particular urgency in the claim (e.g. issues with limitation or a need to act swiftly in the circumstances; but as set out above parents would be sensible to take legal advice as to whether truncating the period for pre-

---

260 Para 16 of the Pre-Action Protocol and see model letter at Annex A to the Pre-Action Protocol

261 Para 16 pf the Pre-Action Protocol

action correspondence and/or an urgent claim is warranted on the particular facts of the case).[262]

If the Defendant fails to respond within the time set out in the pre-action letter, they may face sanctions unless there is good reason for the delay. For this reason, if a Defendant is unable to provide a full response in the time given (e.g. because investigations need to be undertaken and key people are unavailable), it is sensible to send a holding letter acknowledging the letter and proposing a reasonable extension, explaining why it is needed. (This is particularly the case in August, when schools are closed and staff are likely to be away.) The Claimant does not have to agree to the extension, but it is normally sensible to do so provided that there are no limitation difficulties or other reason for urgency.

A reply to a letter before a claim would usually contain the following:

- The public body's response to the claim
- Whether the claim will be resisted in whole or in part
- A copy of the Pre-Action Protocol if the Claimant is a litigant in person[263]

The procedure for bringing a judicial review claim

The procedure for bringing a judicial review claim is governed by CPR Part 54 and PCR PD 54A. Part 54 and the practice directions need to be read in conjunction with Part 8 CPR and section 31 of the Senior Courts Act 1981.

262 Para 20 and model letter at Annex A of the Pre-Action Protocol

263 Para 20 and model letter at Annex A of the Pre-Action Protocol

Making the claim

Applications for judicial review fall within the jurisdiction of the Administrative Court (except for those transferred to be heard by the Upper Tribunal which has its own procedure rules). Judicial review claims involving school exclusions will ordinarily be heard by a single civil judge.

A claim for judicial review is made using the JR claim form (N461), with the additional documentation prescribed in CPR 54.6 and PD 54A. This includes, but is not limited to, a copy of any decision letter or order challenged, a statement of facts and grounds relied upon by the claimant in respect of their claim, which may be inserted in the relevant box in the form or appended separately, and the evidence relied upon in support of the claim).

Claimants have a special duty of disclosure in judicial review claims. They must ensure that they have put all relevant information in their possession before the Court in the application for permission, including any information in their possession that might undermine the claim, rather than just that which supports it. Complying with the duty of candour may involve specifically explaining certain documents or inconsistencies in a witness statement, for example. The duty is a continuing duty, which means that at every stage of proceedings the claimant must consider whether further information requires to be disclosed or explained.

It is very important to check the relevant procedural rules (and the Administrative Court Judicial Review Guide) to ensure that all documentation that is required to go with the claim form has been supplied, otherwise there is a risk of the claim being returned without being issued. Note that the limitation clock does not stop running when a claim form is returned without being issued, and so if the claim form is returned it will be imperative to act quickly to get it back to the Court before the time limit for bringing the claim expires.

Claims may be issued in the Administrative Court Office of the High Court. Once issued, the Claimant must serve a sealed copy of the Claim Form together with the documentation that was filed with it, on the Defendant and any interested parties within 7 days of the claim being issued. The Administrative Court Judicial Review Guide contains further information about the rules relating to service.

Acknowledgment of Service

If the Defendant (or any interested party) wishes to take part in the application for judicial review, they must file and serve an Acknowledgment of Service (AOS) using Form N462. The usual time limit for doing so is 21 days from service of the claim, but this period may be extended or shortened by the Court. If the AOS is not filed within the time limit, the defendant or interested party will not be allowed to take part in the permission stage unless they apply for leave to do so. They may, however, still participate in the substantive hearing if permission is granted.

Reply

New CPR 54.8A(1) gives a claimant who is served with an AOS the right to file a Reply should they wish to do so. According to PD 54A paragraph 7.1(1), any Reply should be filed "only if necessary", e.g. to address something raised in the AOS that was not raised in the claim form. The Reply must be "as concise as possible" and no more than 5 pages long, unless the court gives permission for a longer Reply. The Rules specifically state that the Reply should not be used to rehearse the content of the Claim Form, and that there may be costs consequences if a Reply is filed unnecessarily.

The reply must be filed not more than 7 days after services of the AOS, and served on the defendant and any other person served with the claim form.

Permission of Court required to proceed with the claim

Judicial review claims begin with an application for permission to apply for judicial review, as set out above. In all cases, a single judge will consider the claim on the papers to determine whether all or any of the proposed grounds for judicial review are arguable. The judge may:

- Grant permission on any of the grounds that they consider arguable, on the papers. The judge will also issue directions for preparing for the final hearing, and the case will be listed for a substantive hearing in respect of the grounds for which permission was given.

- List the matter, with directions, for a permission hearing, or for a "rolled up hearing" at which both permission and, if permission is granted, the substantive merits of any grounds permitted to proceed will be determined. A rolled-up hearing may be appropriate where a party has asked for the case to be expedited (common in school exclusions cases) or where the judge takes the view that the case is urgent on the facts.

- Refuse permission. If permission is refused on the basis that the claim is "totally without merit", there is no further right of review in the Administrative Court and the only potential remedy is an appeal to the Court of Appeal. If permission is simply refused, the claimant may file a renewal notice within 7 days seeking a Renewed Permission hearing. If the court refuses permission again at a renewed permission hearing, again there is no further right of review in the Administrative Court and the only potential remedy is an appeal to the Court of Appeal.

Directions

CPR 54.10(1) provides that where permission to proceed is given the court may also give directions.

The contents on these will depend on the nature of the case, but typical directions for a case involving a school exclusion would include: that permission has been granted to apply for Judicial Review, that the Defendant is to now file and serve detailed grounds of resistance and any written evidence, that the Claimant can provide a reply to this alongside further evidence, that the application will be listed on the first available date for a particular time estimate264265'. Directions will also normally include a timetable for filing and serving trial bundles, skeleton arguments and an agreed bundle of authorities.

Evidence and disclosure

Expert evidence

Any party that wishes to rely upon expert evidence (including expert evidence that was served with the claim) must seek the leave of the court.[266]

Disclosure

Disclosure for judicial review claims is not required unless the court orders otherwise.[267] In practice, permission to file further evidence is

264 The reference to the Defendant filing detailed grounds for contesting the claim arises from CPR 54.14. Written evidence can also be provided to support the grounds. CPR 54.14 provides for such a response within 35 days after the order giving permission (unless the Judge has provided for bespoke directions).

265 Typically 3 hours.

266 CPR 35.4. See also *R (Kemp) v Denbighshire Local Health Board* [2006] EWHC 181 (Admin); *BY Development Ltd v Covent Garden Market Authority* [2012] EWHC 2546 (TCC).

267 CPR 54.12. For further discussion of disclosure requirements see Tweed v Parades Commission of Northern Ireland [2007] 1 AC 650.

generally built into the directions rather than the usual civil direction for disclosure. If an application for disclosure is made, it must be "*properly focussed on auditing the legality of public decision-making*".[268] Disclosure may be ordered to make the decision under challenge intelligible.[269] In the exclusions context, it may be necessary to apply for disclosure of Independent Review Panel minutes or governing board meeting minutes if they have not previously been sought or if disclosure has been refused, although efforts should be made to obtain these as part of the pre-action protocol process as set out above.

Witness evidence

Generally speaking, the court does not hear live evidence as part of a judicial review claim. The evidence is generally provided by way of witness statements with documentary exhibits. Whilst the court has an inherent power to hear oral evidence,[270] it will generally only do exceptionally, and where oral evidence is necessary to dispose of the claim fairly and justly.[271] Examples of rare and exceptional situations where live evidence may be appropriate might include a case in which the court requires assistance with expert evidence, or where the case being heard includes a claim under the Human Rights Act (which introduces a more pronounced fact-finding jurisdiction than is usually the case in a claim for judicial review). Parties should also consider carefully if there is any critical factual issue which merits order for cross-examination or disclosure, and seek an appropriate direction at the earliest possible stage.

268 See *R (Bredenkamp v FCO* [2013] EWHC Admin 2480, at para 11.

269 *R (Firstgroup Plc) v Strategic Rail Authority* [2003] EWHC 1611 Admin.

270 *R (PG) v London Borough of Ealing* [2002] ACD 48, per Munby J

271 *R (Bancoult) v Secretary of State for Foreign and Commonwealth Affairs* [2012] EWHC 2115

Remedies

There are six remedies normally available in judicial review, the first three being unique to judicial review:

- **Quashing orders.** A quashing order sets aside the decision that was challenged, so that it has no legal effect. Most commonly, the Court will then remit the matter to the defendant and direct it to reconsider the matter and reach a fresh decision in accordance with the judgment of the Court. Although there are some circumstances in which the Court has the power to substitute its own decision for the decision that has been quashed, this is only in relation to decisions of inferior courts or tribunals, where there has been an error of law, and where there is only one possible decision open to the decision-maker.

- **Mandatory orders.** A mandatory order requires the defendant to do something – for example, to retake a decision in accordance with the law.

- **Prohibiting orders.** A prohibiting order prevents the defendant from taking an action that it has indicated that it intends to take, but has not yet taken.

- **Declarations:** A declaration is a ruling on the rights of the parties or the state of the law. It may be made concerning the way to interpret a piece of legislation in the future, or as to whether an act contemplated by a public body that has not yet been done is lawful or unlawful. They are not granted in respect of hypothetical questions. A declaration is not an order, but there is an expectation that a body will comply with it.

- **Declarations of incompatibility.** These are made where the Court concludes that any Act of Parliament is incompatible with a Convention right. Claimants seeking a declaration of incompatibility must comply with various rules, set out in the Administrative Court Judicial Review Guide, as to the content of their claim form, and as to interested parties to be served with the claim form. The effect of the declaration is to inform Parliament of the incompatibility of the legislation; it does not affect the validity of the legislation concerned.

- **Injunctions**. These are orders compelling the person to whom they are addressed to perform, or refrain from doing, a specific act.

- **Damages:** These are rarely ordered in practice in judicial review proceedings, but are available when:

    - the claimant is seeking another remedy, not just damages alone

    - a private law claim for damages on the same basis would have succeeded if brought in the County Court or appropriate division of the High Court

    - (where damages are sought under the Human Rights Act 1998) the claim for damages has been properly pleaded and particularised.

All remedies in judicial review proceedings are discretionary. The court does not have to grant a remedy, even if the defendant has acted unlawfully, if:

- There was undue delay in filing the application for judicial review, and granting the remedy would be likely to cause substantial hardship to, or substantially prejudice the rights of, any person, or would be detrimental to good administration.[272]

- The error of law was not material to the decision.
- The remedy would serve no useful purpose.
- The claimant has suffered no harm or prejudice.

If the Court considers that the outcome for the Claimant would not have been substantially different if the conduct complained of had not occurred, the Court must refuse to grant any form of relief or damages unless it is appropriate to do so for reasons of exceptional public interest.[273]

Costs

As with other divisions of the High Court, as well as the County Court, legal costs are recoverable by the successful party at the end of the case. A full description of the costs regime is beyond the scope of this work. What should be borne in mind, however, is that the starting point in claims for judicial review is that the successful party is entitled to recover costs that were reasonably incurred and are of a reasonable amount from the unsuccessful party, even if the latter is not themselves represented. The Court has discretion to depart from this in appropriate cases, but a privately funded or self-representing claimant runs the risk of having to pay their own costs and the reasonable costs of the other side if they lose and costs can be substantial. Anyone contemplating a claim for judicial review should seek early advice as to the merits of the claim, the funding options available, and the risk in relation to costs if unsuccessful.

---

272 Senior Courts Act 1981 section 31(6)(b)

273 Senior Courts Act 1981 section 31(2A) and (2B)

Conclusion

As can be seen, judicial review is a niche remedy that may in some cases be the only option for remedying legal errors in the decisions of Independent Review Panels or governing bodies reconsidering an exclusion following an Independent Review Panel hearing. However, it is limited in practice, because the court's powers are limited to scrutinising the decision and requiring the decision-maker to re-take it. In many cases, even after a judicial review has succeeded, and even where the court has been highly critical of the way in which the decision was taken, it will still be possible for the Independent Review Panel or governors to make a decision that has the same effect as the decision that was found to be unlawful, whilst applying the law correctly.

In the context of disabled pupils, the Upper Tribunal has recently considered whether judicial review is the right remedy in the majority of cases concerning disabled children:

> *"But it is surely not proportionate for a parent to have to bring a claim in the courts for judicial review (risking an adverse decision on costs and being subject to a much more formal regime) rather than simply appealing to the expert, informal First-tier Tribunal, relying on the provisions of the Equality Act. Dr. Armstrong highlighted the potential absurdity and disproportionality of parents first having to appeal to the First-tier Tribunal for a determination on whether their child had a 'tendency to physical abuse' and then, if it was found that they had, having to bring a further claim for judicial review. I accept the submission made both by Dr. Armstrong and Mr. Broach that judicial review does not provide a practical, effective facility for testing the proportionality of the exclusion in cases such as these."*[274]

[274] *C & C v The Governing Body of a School, The Secretary of State for Education (First Interested Party) and The National Autistic Society (Second Interested Party) (SEN)*: [2018] UKUT 269 (AAC) at Para 84

Chapter 6 deals with cases involving discrimination claims arising from school exclusions.

Further reading

The Administrative Court has produced a comprehensive guide to practice and procedure in claims for judicial review, called The Administrative Court Judicial Review Guide. The latest edition at the time of publication was the 2023 edition and it is available online. It is required reading (at the earliest possible stage) for anyone contemplating representing themselves in a claim for judicial review, along with the other resources mentioned in previous chapters.

CHAPTER FIVE

INDEPENDENT SCHOOLS

Overview

In this chapter, we look briefly at the position of a pupil who has been excluded from an independent school.[275]

We have seen that pupils in state schools have significant procedural safeguards in place in the event that the head teacher decides to exclude them, as well as two potential avenues of appeal: to the Board of Governors, and then from the Board of Governors to the Independent Review Panel, with the possibility of a claim for judicial review of the Independent Review Panel's decision.

Pupils in independent schools are in a very different position. It is firmly established that the decision of an independent school to exclude is not a public law decision and is not amenable to judicial review.[276] The relationship between an independent school and its pupil is one of private law, regulated by the contract between the school and the parents (although the school obviously does owe other duties directly to pupils, e.g. various statutory duties and generally in tort). Note, however, that

---

[275] As defined by section 463 Education Act 1996 as amended: any school providing full-time education to 5 or more pupils of compulsory school age, or at least one pupil of compulsory school age for whom an EHC plan/statement of special educational needs is maintained, or who is looked after by a local authority, and which is not a school maintained by a local authority or a non-maintained special school. Note that independent schools must satisfy the Independent School Standards as a condition of registration.

[276] *R v Incorporated Froebel Institute, ex p L [1999] ELR 488, QBD; R v Headmaster of Fernhill Manor School, ex p Brown* (1992) Times 5th June

independent schools are bound by the terms of the Equality Act 2010, and therefore a discriminatory decision to exclude may give rise to remedies under the Equality Act 2010 even if it is not strictly in breach of the contract – see below and Chapter 6.

Limited involvement of public law in the independent sector

In Chapter 4, we looked at the very limited role of public law principles in the independent education sector. The absence of any public law framework in relation to exclusions in independent schools means that the range of legitimate grounds for exclusion in the independent sector is wider than those available to head teachers in the state sector. It cannot be said that public law principles are completely irrelevant, but fundamentally the question is what the contract permits. An independent school may exclude a pupil for:

- A serious breach or breaches by the pupil of the school's behaviour/discipline policy;

- A breach of contract by the *parent* (a marked departure from the position of the state school pupil – in our experience, independent schools are increasingly requiring parents to give undertakings as to their own behaviour as well as their child's, meaning that a parent who behaves aggressively or unreasonably towards teachers on or off-site may put their child at risk of exclusion even if the child's behaviour is exemplary);

- Failure of the pupil to meet the school academic standards, or (as some contracts say) where the head teacher is of the view that the pupil is unable to benefit from the education and facilities offered by the school.

There is no standard contract used by independent schools – each provider will have its own contract – and therefore the terms of the specific contract between the school and the parents will be of paramount importance in deciding whether an exclusion is lawful. Frequently, a contract with an independent school will make provision for the head teacher to use his or her discretion to exclude on two broad grounds:

- A power to exclude (or expel) a pupil, usually where the pupil has committed misconduct or in some way behaved in a manner that is inconsistent with the School's disciplinary policy;
- A power to require parents to remove a pupil, where the head teacher feels that the pupil is unable to meet the School's academic standards or otherwise to benefit from the facilities and provision that the School can provide, or where the parent's behaviour has fallen short of the contractual standards agreed.

Safeguards

These are mostly contractual. A full description of the operation of commercial and contract law is beyond the scope of this work, but broadly:

- Any express terms in the contract providing rights to the parent or pupil – for example, an express term providing for a right of appeal. If the contract does not provide a specific right of appeal against a decision to exclude, parents may be able to use the school's general complaints procedure to achieve a review of the decision by governors or trustees.
- The power to exclude is generally expressed as a discretion to be exercised by the head teacher under the contract. A contractual discretion must be exercised reasonably (although it will always be difficult to persuade a court to intervene in the absence of very obviously unreasonable decision-making or conduct).

- All contracts for the provision of services (including contracts for the provision of education) are deemed by law[277] to contain an implied term that the school will carry out its duties under the contract with reasonable care and skill. "Implied" means that the contract is deemed to contain this term even if it does not appear in the contract. It is unlawful to seek to seek to exclude liability for failure to perform with reasonable skill and care.

- The Consumer Rights Act 2015[278] protects consumers from unfair contract terms. A term is unfair if it "*causes a significant imbalance in the parties' rights and obligations under the contract, to the detriment of the consumer*",[279] having regard to the circumstances at the time that the term was agreed; the other terms of the contract, or any other connected contract; and what is being provided under the contract.[280] Contractual terms must be transparent, simple to understand, not take advantage of a consumer's vulnerability, and should take into account a consumer's legitimate interests.

---

277 Supply of Goods and Services Act 1982, section 13 (for contracts entered into prior to October 2015); Consumer Rights Act 2015, section 49 (for contracts entered into after October 2015); but note that there were also a number of amendments and refinements to both Acts before and after 2015.

278 For contracts entered into after October 2015; for contracts entered into prior to that date, broadly similar (but less extensive) statutory protections were contained across a number of different Acts including the Supply of Goods and Services Act 1982, the Unfair Contract Terms Act 1977 ("UCTA") and the Unfair Terms in Consumer Contract Regulations 1999 ("UTCCR"). Note that there were a number of amendments and refinements to these Acts over time.

279 Consumer Rights Act 2015, section 62(4)

280 Consumer Rights Act 2015, section 62(5)

- There is a general expectation that head teachers will observe principles of natural justice in investigating a conduct offence against a pupil (and, arguably, against a parent, although there has been no case on that point to date).

However, in practice the courts have shown themselves to be extremely reluctant to issue injunctions preventing independent schools from excluding pupils.[281] Whether or not a pupil is entitled to an appeal hearing is a matter of contract, not of public law.[282]

Record-keeping

In Chapter 2 we set out a list of matters that a tribunal scrutinising an exclusion is likely to expect to have been documented by the school. Although Chapter 2 relates largely to maintained schools, that expectation applies as much to independent schools as to maintained schools and academies. The scope for exclusion or requiring removal under a contract in the private sector will be wider, of course, but nonetheless a contractual dispute may arise between school and parents; a tortious dispute may arise; a discrimination claim may be brought. In all of these eventualities, such records will be relevant in relation to the head teacher's decision to exclude a pupil, or to require the pupil to be removed by their parents. Regardless of the reason for exclusion or removal, the head teacher should ensure that the reasons why the exclusion or request to remove has been made are fully documented, and should at the same time satisfy themselves that these are in accordance with the contract and are not discriminatory (see Chapter 6). The head teacher should also fully document any investigation that has been necessary, or ensure that whoever carries out the investigation does so.

281 *Gray v Marlborough College* [2006] EWCA Civ 1262

282 *M v W* [2006] EWHC 575 (QB)

Remedies for breach of contract

A full consideration of the range of remedies available for breach of contract are beyond the scope of this work. However, such remedies tend to be linked to financial loss, and for these reasons are likely to be of limited value in claims relating to exclusions, where the real impact is psychological or reputational rather than financial. In theory one potential remedy for breach of contract – either on an interim basis or as part of the final disposal of the case – is an injunction. However, in practice, the civil courts have been unwilling to grant injunctions preventing head teachers from excluding pupils, or requiring head teachers to reinstate excluded pupils. Damages for breach of contract are always going to be difficult to identify and quantify but may include a partial refund of fees; the cost of having to purchase new school uniform; costs incidental to having to attend a new school, and so on. There will of course be a duty to mitigate any financial loss where possible.

Discriminatory exclusions

Independent schools have a duty under the Equality Act 2010 not to discriminate against pupils, just as state schools do. Accordingly, if a pupil's exclusion is tainted by discrimination or other unlawful conduct under the Equality Act 2010, they may bring a claim against the school under that Act. Remedies open to courts and tribunals under the Equality Act 2010 include the power to direct reinstatement of a pupil, financial compensation (unless the claim is a claim for disability discrimination being heard in the First-tier Tribunal) and other powers such as requiring a school to undergo training or to provide an apology. We discuss discrimination claims in more detail in Chapter 6.

Conclusion

Pupils in independent schools who have been excluded for non-discriminatory reasons have much more limited scope for redress in the event of an unfair exclusion, because the relationship with the school is governed by the contractual terms agreed between the parties. There is no automatic right to an appeal or review and no scope for judicial review. However, parents may submit a complaint to Ofsted/the Independent Schools Inspectorate. This will not be investigated individually, but may, if appropriate, form part of the intelligence for any subsequent inspection.

CHAPTER SIX

DISCRIMINATION

Introduction and Overview

In Chapters 2 and 3, we looked at the decision-making process of the head teacher, and at the statutory mechanism for review of that decision by the governing board and the Independent Review Panel. We saw that even if the Independent Review Panel considers that a decision to exclude was flawed (including a finding that the exclusion was discriminatory under the Equality Act), its powers of redress are limited. The most that it can do is force the governing board to reconsider the decision to exclude, with limited financial sanctions in the event that the governing body refuses to do so. It cannot order a school to reinstate a pupil who has been unlawfully excluded; nor can the Administrative Court on an application for judicial review, as we saw in Chapter 4. In Chapter 5, we saw that public law principles have at best limited application in the independent sector, where contract is king. Principles of commercial contract do not always feel like the best fit with the welfare of children.

Where, however, an exclusion is not just unjustified, but discriminatory, a further and more satisfactory route to redress may be available. Schools – including independent schools – are prohibited by the Equality Act 2010 (referred to hereafter in this chapter as "the Act") from unlawfully discriminating against pupils (or prospective pupils). This includes an explicit duty not to discriminate against a pupil by excluding the pupil from the school.[283] Claims for discrimination against schools are heard in the County Court, the only exception being disability discrimination claims, which are heard by the First-tier Tribunal. These venues are not limited to public law principles or principles of contract. They will hear

283 Equality Act 2010, section 85(2)(e)

all of the relevant evidence produced by the parties, and decide whether, as a matter of fact, the exclusion was tainted by discrimination. If it did, then they have various powers available to them, including the power to order reinstatement. The County Court also has the power to award financial compensation, which is not within the power of the First-tier Tribunal.

We should add, of course, that other acts or omissions by schools apart from exclusions may be discriminatory and may form the basis of a claim under the Act; but obviously this book is particularly concerned with decisions to exclude.

It is important, therefore, that parents, schools and local authorities understand how the Act works and when it might be appropriate to bring a claim for discrimination under the Act. In this chapter we,

- summarise the key concepts of the Act
- review the remedies available under the Act
- examine some previously decided cases relating to discriminatory exclusions.

History and Territorial Jurisdiction

Prior to 2010, anti-discrimination law was set out in a number of different Acts of Parliament and associated statutory instruments. The Act consolidated and replaced this legislation, but also clarified the law and extended protection in some areas. Cases decided under the previous regime will not necessarily be irrelevant, but should be treated with some caution.

The Act applies to England, Wales and Scotland. Note that due to devolution there are some operational differences in the way that the Act works in England, Scotland and Wales. Where this is the case, the Act sets out separate requirements or exceptions for the particular jurisdiction.

The Act does not apply in Northern Ireland, and so parents wishing to bring a discrimination claim against a school would need to take separate advice.

Key concepts under the Equality Act

Summary

The Act sets out and defines a number of "protected characteristics" – broadly, these are characteristics that people cannot choose to have or not have (although there will always be some controversy about this in relation to, for example, religious or philosophical belief). Nine are defined altogether, but it is important to be aware that only seven of them apply in relation to schools: disability, gender reassignment, pregnancy and maternity (technically a form of prohibited conduct, but generally included in the list of prohibited characteristics), race, religion or belief, sex, and sexual orientation. Age discrimination is not a protected characteristic so far as schools are concerned, because schools need to be able to treat pupils differently from each other depending on their age. Matrimonial status is also not a protected characteristic for the purposes of education.

Having set out the protected characteristics, the Act then set out a list of forms of conduct which are unlawful when they happen because of a person's protected characteristic:

- Direct discrimination (section 13)
- Indirect discrimination (section 19)
- Harassment (section 26)

- Victimisation (section 27)
- Failure to comply with the duty to make reasonable adjustments for disabled people (sections 20-22)
- Discrimination arising from disability (section 15)
- Pregnancy and maternity discrimination (section 17, for schools)

The Act then goes on to set out the areas of activity in which the prohibited conduct described in Part 2 will be unlawful. These are: services (Part 3), premises (Part 4), work (Part 5), education (Part 6: see below), and associations (Part 7). Specific rules in relation to disabled persons and transport are set out in Part 12. The public sector equality duty (PSED), to which schools are subject, and which is touched upon at the end of this chapter, is set out in Part 11.

It will be clear that schools will have duties in relation to pupils and prospective pupils under Part 6; in relation to employees and workers under Part 5; and in relation to recipients of services under Part 3. They may also have duties in relation to premises under Part 4. For the purposes of this book, we are primarily interested in their duties under Part 6.

The Act also sets out a regime for enforcement (Part 9), i.e. where to bring a claim for discrimination; the time limit for bringing such a claim; and the powers available to the court or tribunal if the claim succeeds.

Schools, Responsible Bodies of schools, and pupils

Chapter 1 of Part 6 applies to all schools in England and Wales. These are:

- schools (mainstream or special) maintained by local authorities
- independent educational institutions (other than special schools);

- alternative provision academies that are not independent educational institutions; and

- special schools that are not maintained by local authorities.[284]

Slightly different provisions apply in Scotland.[285]

Part 6 of the Act places a duty upon responsible bodies of schools in relation to pupils and prospective pupils. All of these terms have statutory definitions, mostly deriving from the Education Act 1996:

- "School" means an educational institution outside of the further education sector and the higher education sector, which is an institution for providing primary and/or secondary education and is not a 16 to 19 Academy.[286]

- "Pupil" means a person aged 18 or under for whom education is being provided at a school (unless it is part-time education suitable for persons over compulsory school age).[287]

- The identity of the Responsible Body (often referred to as the RB) will depend upon the type of school involved:[288]

    - Independent schools, non-maintained special schools and academies: the proprietor.

---

284 Equality Act 2010, section 85(7)

285 Equality Act 2010, section 85(8) and see also section 85(9)

286 Education Act 1996, section 4(1)–(1B)

287 Education Act 1996, section 3(1)

288 Equality Act 2010, section 85(9)

- Maintained schools in England and Wales: the local authority or governing board.

- Pupil Referral Units (PRUs): the local authority.

Protected Characteristics[289]

Schools are not permitted to discriminate against, or engage in other prohibited conduct in relation to, pupils or prospective pupils with the following protected characteristics:

- Disability
- Gender reassignment
- Pregnancy and maternity[290]
- Race
- Religion or belief
- Sex
- Sexual orientation

As previously noted, age and marital status are not protected characteristics in the schools context.

289 *Technical Guidance for Schools,* EHRC, paragraphs 5.102-5.129

290 This is not listed as a protected characteristic – the Act treats discrimination in relation to pregnancy and maternity as a discrete form of prohibited conduct – but it is obviously a protected characteristic by implication.

Disability

Summary

A pupil is disabled within the meaning of the Act if they have:

- a physical or mental impairment
- which has a substantial and long-term adverse effect on the pupil's ability to
- carry out normal day-to-day activities.[291]

We see a high volume of disability discrimination claims brought against schools. In most cases there will be little dispute as to whether a pupil is disabled, particularly if they are already receiving special educational provision at school. If a pupil is receiving special educational provision via an EHC Plan it is even more likely that they will quality as disabled. However, in a minority of cases there can be a dispute as to whether or not a pupil is disabled, and so it is important to understand the factors that are relevant in deciding whether or not a pupil meets the definition.

Physical or mental impairment

The Act does not contain an exhaustive list of recognised illnesses or conditions that will always amount to a disability (although a select minority of conditions will always amount to an impairment, as set out below). Nor does it require a pupil to have a formal or recognised diagnosis of their condition in order to meet the definition of "disabled". All that is required, as a starting point, is a physical or mental impairment (a phrase that has been found to bear its ordinary and natural meaning).[292] Whether or not a particular individual has an impairment

---

[291] Equality Act 2010, section 6(1)

[292] *McNicol v Balfour Beatty Rail Maintenance Ltd* [2002] ICR 1498, CA

is a matter for a court or tribunal to decide on the evidence before it. Frequently pupils will have a formal diagnosis, and it is helpful if they do, but that is not always the case.

> *Priya is 7. Her school has observed that for the past two years, despite extra help in class, she has been and remains significantly behind her peers in literacy and numeracy, that she appears to struggle with making and keeping friendships, and that she exhibits sensory difficulties. As a result Priya frequently needs time out of class and assistance to help her regulate her emotions. She is also receiving a differentiated curriculum. Priya was referred for a multidisciplinary assessment for ASD, which confirmed Priya's difficulties but found that she did not meet the criteria for a diagnosis of ASD. The school cannot conclude that Priya is not disabled simply because the MDT declined to put a label on the symptoms that were recorded in the report and which the school had observed itself.*

A diagnosis of ASD will qualify as a mental impairment. However, if Priya's parents brought a claim before the First-tier Tribunal, and if the Tribunal was satisfied that she exhibited cognitive difficulties, sensory processing issues and difficulties with social communication, that would in principle be sufficient for it to conclude that Priya had a mental or physical impairment. It may be impossible to find a formal diagnosis of the underlying cause of those symptoms; that does not matter, as long as the evidence shows that there is an impairment, diagnosed or not, that has the requisite severity and duration of effect.

This also means that there are (with a few statutory exceptions which we will come to shortly) no hard and fast rules about whether or not a particular impairment amounts to a disability or not. One pupil may have anxiety that does not amount to a disability; another pupil may have anxiety that does amount to a disability. The question is always whether there is an impairment, and how the impairment affects the individual.

Conditions that are never impairments

For public policy reasons, the following conditions are not to be treated as impairments, regardless of the severity and duration of their effect upon the individual:

- Alcoholism, nicotine addiction and addiction to any other substance that was not initially medically prescribed.[293]
- A tendency to set fires or to steal, exhibitionism, and voyeurism.
- A tendency to physical or sexual abuse of other persons[294]

The public policy behind these exceptions is fairly obvious. However, the tendency to physical abuse has proved controversial. In X v Governing Body of a School (SEN) [2015] UKUT 0007 (AAC), a primary school pupil with a diagnosis of autism was permanently excluded from school after a series of violent outbursts involving physical harm to other pupils and teachers. The pupil's parents brought a claim for disability discrimination. The First-tier Tribunal found that the pupil had a tendency to physical abuse of other persons and that this was because of her autism. They found that Regulation 4 prohibited them from treating her condition as an impairment. The Upper Tribunal agreed. This obviously made it much easier for schools to exclude children for physically abusive conduct that arose from their underlying disability.

This point was revisited in 2018, in the case of C & C v Governing Body of a School [2018] UKUT 269 (AAC). The pupil had been subjected to a fixed-period exclusion (previously known as a suspension) for behaviour which was physically abusive of others. The child had autism, anxiety,

293 Equality Act 2010 (Disability) Regulations 2010 (SI 2010/2028), Regulation 3

294 Equality Act 2010 (Disability) Regulations 2010 (SI 2010/2028), Regulation 4

and pathological demand avoidance. The First-tier Tribunal accepted that the behaviour arose from the child's underlying disability and that she had a tendency to physically abuse others, so found that Regulation 4(c) prevented her claim from succeeding. On appeal, however, the Upper Tribunal found that Regulation 4(1)(c) was incompatible with Article 14 (read with Article 2 of Protocol 1, the right to education) of the ECHR. This was because the effect of Regulation 4(c) is to treat children whose disability manifests in physically abusive behaviour differently from children whose disability does not. This difference in treatment could not be justified where it resulted in the removal of a remedy from children for a discriminatory exclusion in the courts. Regulation 4(1)(c) has not, at the time of writing, been amended or repealed by the government, but most cases proceed on the basis that the Upper Tribunal's judgment is correct.

This was a victory for disabled children and their parents, but it is important to understand the limitations of the decision. First, parents will need to be able to show that the physically abusive behaviour for which the child was excluded arose from their disability. This is not always easy to prove, although it may feel obvious to a parent who is familiar with the effects of a disability upon their child. The fact that a child has autism or PDA, for example, does not necessarily mean that the behaviour for which they were excluded is intrinsic to their underlying disability or that it is beyond their ability to control. In some cases, a Tribunal may be prepared to infer this from other evidence, and in others it may not. Note also that if the child's physically abusive behaviour is intrinsic to their disability, their school may still be able to argue that the exclusion was legally justified (a concept explained later in this chapter).

Andrew, 15, has high-functioning ASD with associated social communication and attention issues. He has no documented PDA traits and none of his social communication difficulties have led to fights or altercations with other pupils. He is on course to gain top marks across the board in his GCSEs. One day Andrew suggests to his friends that they start a water fight with another group of boys after school. During the water fight, Andrew pushes one boy to the floor and punches him repeatedly, breaking his nose. There is no record of difficulties with the other boy and Andrew says he "got carried away". Andrew's parents believe that it is obvious that this behaviour arose from Andrew's disability. However, it would be very risky to bring a claim for disability discrimination without evidence from an expert supporting that conclusion.

Lisa has ASD, ADHD, severe sensory processing issues, and falls somewhere between moderate and severe learning difficulties. She is non-verbal. At her school, a specialist setting for MLD students, Lisa can become highly anxious in class. When she does so she may lash out at teachers and attack or throw things at staff or peers who try to approach her. The school was not aware when it agreed to be named in Lisa's EHC Plan that she required a quiet room to be available as this was not in her Plan; it does not have a quiet room, meaning that every time Lisa becomes physically challenging her class has to be evacuated to the playground. The school excluded Lisa when these incidents started to happen two or three times per week. We think that the Tribunal would be more likely to accept, on these facts, that Lisa's physically abusive behaviour was intrinsically linked to her disabilities (although we would still always advise that expert evidence be obtained for the claim). The school may still be able to justify an exclusion if they can show that they have a legitimate aim (e.g. safeguarding their staff and pupils from harm) and that there were no reasonable steps short of permanent exclusion that they could take to keep staff safe at school.

Conditions that are always to be treated as impairments

The following will always be treated as impairments:

- cancer, HIV infection, and multiple sclerosis;[295]
- severe disfigurement (not including tattoos or body piercings that have not been removed);[296]
- visual impairment, where the pupil is certified as blind, severely sight impaired, sight impaired or partially sighted by a consultant ophthalmologist.[297]

Substantial and adverse effect

Substantial means more than minor or trivial. The impairment must have a substantial and adverse long-term effect upon the pupil's ability to carry out day-to-day activities. However, "substantial adverse effect" must not be taken to mean that the pupil has to be incapable of carrying out day-to-day activities. Disabled people adapt in order to manage their conditions, and disabled pupils are no exception. Steps that disabled people might take to manage their conditions could include avoiding particular day-to-day activities because they cause pain, fatigue or social embarrassment, or because of a loss of energy or motivation. The impairment and its effect may make it harder or more time-consuming for a disabled pupil to carry out an activity, compared to someone who does not have the impairment.[298]

---

295 Equality Act 2010, Schedule 1, para. 6(1)

296 Equality Act 2010, Schedule 1, para 3, and Equality Act 2010 (Disability) Regulations 2010, Regulation 5

297 Equality Act 2010 (Disability) Regulations 2010, Regulation 7

298 *Goodwin v Patent Office* [1999] ICR 302, EAT

In addition:

- A pupil who was disabled in the past will be treated as disabled even if the condition has completely resolved itself.[299]

- A pupil with a disability that has resolved, but in respect of which the substantial and adverse long-term effect is likely to recur in the future, will be treated as disabled.[300]

- Where a pupil has a progressive condition, which affects/has affected the pupil's ability to carry out normal day to day activities, but not yet substantially, the pupil will be treated as having an impairment that has a substantial adverse effect if the condition is likely to result in them having one.[301]

- If a child under 6 years old has an impairment, which does not have a substantial and long-term effect on their ability to carry out normal day to day activities, but would have that effect on a person aged 6 years or over, the impairment will be treated as having that effect.[302]

- In deciding whether a pupil has an impairment that has a substantial adverse effect, any treatment or auxiliary aids, adaptations, assistance, etc that mitigate the effect have to be discounted. If, but for that treatment/aid/assistance, the impairment would have a substantial adverse effect, the impairment will be treated as having that effect[303] (unless it is an impairment of sight, in which case it is the effect whilst the

299 Equality Act 2010, section 6(4)

300 Equality Act 2010, Schedule 1, para. 2(2)

301 Equality Act 2010, Schedule 1, para 8

302 Equality Act 2010 (Disability) Regulations 2010, Regulation 6

303 Equality Act 2010, Schedule 1, para. 5(1)

person is wearing glasses/contact lenses/some other means of correction that is taken into account).[304]

Mark has ADHD which severely affected his ability to participate in classes. He has been on stimulant medication for the last four months and his teachers now describe him as lively, but generally hard-working and no longer disruptive. It would be a mistake, however, for the school to cease to treat Mark as disabled under the Act, because without medication his condition would continue to have a substantial and adverse effect upon his ability to carry out normal day to day activities.

Long-term effect

The effect of the impairment must also be long-term, which means that it must:

- Have lasted for at least 12 months
- Be likely to last for at least 12 months in total, or
- Last for the rest of the pupil's life.

As set out above, if the person no longer has the condition, or if they currently do not have the condition but it is likely to recur, they will still be considered to be a disabled person under the Act.

[304] Equality Act 2010, Schedule 1, para. 5(3)

> *Renata is 15. She was diagnosed with generalised anxiety disorder at 10 and was under the care of CAMHS for six months. A combination of counselling and medication was highly effective and apart from a brief relapse 18 months ago she has experienced no further symptoms. However, her consultant was of the view on discharge that her symptoms are likely to recur. The school should work on the basis that Renata is still disabled within the meaning of the Act despite the fact that she has been symptom-free for a year and a half.*

Ability to carry out day-to-day activities

"Normal-day-to-day activities" are activities that are carried out by most people on a fairly regular and frequent basis. Good examples of these are walking, writing, concentrating, climbing stairs, etc. It is not intended to mean hobbies like piano playing, knitting, or rugby, as these are not carried out by most people on a regular and frequent basis (although if a pupil's manual dexterity or ability to mobilise is affected that will obviously affect their ability to participate in pastimes that they enjoy). However, the definition is also capable of covering activities that many people will do at least once, such as a high-pressure examination, which has been held (in the employment law context) to constitute a normal day-to-day activity even though most people do not take examinations on a daily or weekly basis.

Knowledge and constructive knowledge of disability

A responsible body may have a defence to a claim for discrimination arising from disability if it can show that it did not know, and could not reasonably have been expected to know, that the pupil had the disability in question.[305] These states of knowledge are often referred to as "actual knowledge" (i.e. the school is aware that the pupil has a mental or

---

305 Equality Act 2010, section 15(2); see also *Technical guidance for schools*, EHRC, paragraph 5.50-5.52

physical impairment that has a substantial and adverse effect on their ability to carry out normal day-to-day activities, and that this has lasted or is likely to last more than 12 months), and "constructive knowledge". A school is expected to do everything that it reasonably can to find out if a pupil has a disability, and may be considered to have constructive knowledge of a disability if

- it has not done everything that it reasonably could do in the circumstances to establish whether or not the pupil has a disability, and
- if it had followed all reasonable lines of enquiry, having done so it could reasonably have been expected to know that the pupil had the disability in question.[306]

Danny, 12, has stress, depression and a significant attachment disorder. His parents do not accept these diagnoses and are concerned that they and Danny will be stigmatised. They move to a different area and do not disclose any disabilities to Danny's new school. Within four weeks the SENCo of the local Academy that Danny attends contacts Danny's parents to say that his teachers are very concerned about his behaviour, that he is already at risk of exclusion, and that the school would like him to undergo some assessments. The parents refuse to agree to an assessment or to any involvement from CAMHS or the school counsellor, or to obtain their own private assessment. The school alerts the Local Authority, which is also unable to persuade parents to agree. If Danny is ultimately excluded for behaviour that arises out of the disabilities that were withheld from the school, it is likely that the school would be able to show that they had followed all reasonable lines of inquiry to determine whether or not Danny had a disability.

306 *A Ltd v Z* [2019] UKEAT 0273_18_2803 (28th March 2019)

This defence of lack of knowledge is not extended to claims for direct or indirect discrimination, or to harassment or victimisation (although evidentially the employer's knowledge or lack thereof is likely to be relevant).

Gender reassignment

A pupil has this protected characteristic if they are

- proposing to undergo, or
- are undergoing, or
- have undergone

a process, or part of a process, for the purpose of reassigning their sex by changing physiological or other attributes of sex.[307] The Act refers to a person who has this protected characteristic as a transsexual.

A child can have the protected characteristic of gender reassignment.[308]

Pregnancy and maternity[309]

A pupil who is pregnant, regardless of their age, is protected from discrimination because she:

---

307 Equality Act 2010, section 7(1); see also *Technical Guidance for* Schools, EHRC, paragraph 5.112-4

308 Technical guidance for schools in England, last updated July 2024, at 5.116.

309 *Technical Guidance for Schools,* EHRC, updated July 2024 paragraphs from page 48

- is or has been pregnant[310]

- has given birth in the last 26 weeks (whether to a living child or to a stillborn child);[311] or

- is breastfeeding a baby who is 26 weeks or younger.[312]

Race

Race includes colour, nationality and ethnic or national origins.[313] This is non-exhaustive: in the employment context "race" has been held to include the status in the caste system of an Indian national.[314] "Ethnic origins" has been held to incorporate "descent"[315]. Racial grounds can comprise two or more racial groups.[316]

Religion or belief

Religion or belief includes:[317]

- Any religion

- Any religious or philosophical belief

---

310 Equality Act 2010, section 17(2)

311 Equality Act 2010, section 17(3)

312 Equality Act 2010, section 17(3)

313 Equality Act 2010, section 9(1)

314 *Chandhok and anor v Tirkey* [2015] ICR 527, EAT

315 *R (on the application of E) v Governing Body of JFS and the Admissions Appeal Panel of JFS and ors* [2010] IRLR 136, SC

316 Equality Act 2010, section 9(4)

317 Equality Act 2010, section 10

- A lack of any such religion or belief

In order to be protected, a religion must:[318]

- Be identifiable (it does not need to be well-known or mainstream)
- Have a clear structure and belief system
- Be a religion in its own right, or a denomination/sect within a religion

A religious belief goes beyond beliefs about and adherence to a religion or its central articles of faith, and may vary from person to person within the same religion.[319]

A belief which is not a religious belief:[320]

- May be a philosophical belief (e.g. atheism)
- Need not include faith or worship, but must affect the way in which a person lives their life and perceives the world
- Must be genuine[321]
- Must be a belief rather than an information-based opinion

---

318 *Technical Guidance for* Schools, EHRC, paragraph 5.121-5.122

319 *Technical Guidance for* Schools, EHRC, paragraph 5.122

320 *Grainger plc and ors v Nicholson* [2010] ICR 360 EAT; see also *Technical Guidance for* Schools, EHRC, paragraph 5.125

321 *Grainger,* op.cit

- Must be a belief as to a weighty and substantial aspect of human life and behaviour
- Must attain a certain level of cogency, seriousness, cohesion and importance
- Must be worthy of respect in a democratic society
- Must be compatible with human dignity, and not conflict with the fundamental rights of others.

Sex

A person's sex refers to the fact that they are male or female. In relation to a group of people, it refers to either men or women or to boys or girls.[322]

Sexual orientation

Sexual orientation[323] means a person's attraction towards:

5. Persons of the same sex
6. Persons of the opposite sex, or
7. Persons of either sex.

Prohibited conduct

The Act identifies and prohibits a number of forms of discriminatory behaviour and associated unlawful conduct. If a school discriminates

322 Equality Act 2010, section 11

323 Equality Act 2010, section 12

against a pupil, or engages in other unlawful conduct against them under the Act, a claim may be brought against the school under the Act.

Direct discrimination[324]

Direct discrimination occurs when a school:

- treats a pupil less favourably than it treats, or would treat, another pupil,[325] and
- the difference in treatment is because of a protected characteristic.

> *Luke, a black British pupil of Jamaican descent, is the best debater in his school and has an impeccable disciplinary and academic record. Luke's English teacher wants to make him the captain of the debating team. The head teacher overrules her and chooses a white British pupil instead, saying that Luke will not "fit in" at external debating competitions. The head teacher is unable to explain what he means by this.*

Some forms of discrimination can be justified, as we will shortly see. Direct discrimination is not one of them. It is always unlawful and can never be justified.[326] Single-sex schools and religious schools are able to continue to operate because of specific statutory exceptions rendering them lawful; in the absence of those exceptions it would be directly discriminatory to run a single-sex school or a religious school.

---

324 Equality Act 2010, section 13; see also *Technical Guidance for Schools*, ECHR, paragraph 5.3–5.10

325 Equality Act 2010, section 13

326 Outside of the school's sphere, direct age discrimination is capable of being justified, but as discussed above age is not a relevant protected characteristic in relation to schools.

Note that discrimination that is well-intentioned but misguided is still unlawful if it results in less favourable treatment.

> *Lila has cerebral palsy. This affects her voice, making her sound breathless and high-pitched. She is very keen to participate in all areas of the curriculum and particularly loves Drama. However, her Drama teacher ignores her hand when asking for volunteers to perform in front of the class because he believes that performing is too taxing for her and that he is doing her a kindness by sparing her the effort. This constitutes direct discrimination regardless of the teacher's motivation.*

Less favourable treatment/comparators

In order to prove direct discrimination, it is necessary to show that the claimant was subjected to "less favourable treatment" by the school. There are only two exceptions to this:

- Where the complaint is direct discrimination due to racial segregation, which is always unlawful direct discrimination; and

- Where the complaint is direct discrimination due to pregnancy or maternity. In this instance the requirement is unfavourable treatment (i.e. not by comparison to anyone else), rather than less favourable treatment.

This means that a claimant in a discrimination claim must compare the way that they have been treated, to the way that a person is being treated, or would be treated, if they did not have the claimant's protected characteristic.[327] So if the claim is brought by a male for direct sex discrimination, the comparator will be female; if the claim is brought by

327 *Technical Guidance for* Schools, EHRC, paragraph 5.5–6

a straight pupil for direct discrimination because of sexual orientation, the comparator will be gay or bisexual; and so on.

> *A group consisting of three boys and a girl are disrupting a class by talking loudly and pushing each other out of their chairs. The teacher sends the boys to the head teacher, but only verbally reprimands the girl. The teacher cannot explain why she did not send the girl out too.*

The comparator can be an actual comparator, or a hypothetical comparator. Whichever is chosen, there must be no material difference between the circumstances relating to the comparator and the circumstances relating to the pupil. Any material difference between the cases can result in the chosen comparator not being valid. It is usually sensible for a pupil who thinks they have identified an actual comparator to rely on a hypothetical comparator in the alternative (i.e. as a Plan B if the court or tribunal does not accept the proposed actual comparator as valid.)

> *One of the boys in the above example, Mark, brings a claim for direct sex discrimination. He argues in court that the girl is an actual comparator in relation to whom he was treated less favourably and that the only reason he was treated less favourably was his sex. The school argues that the girl's situation is materially different because, unlike Mark and the other two boys who have poor behaviour records, it was her first offence and it would not have been reasonable to send her to the head teacher.*

In this scenario, Mark would probably want to make the evidential point that if that was the explanation it's hard to see why the teacher wasn't able to say so at the time. But Mark could also argue, in the alternative, that a hypothetical comparator (i.e. a girl who had a poor behaviour record comparable to his) would not have been sent to the Head. This might involve calling evidence as to how other people in the class had been treated in the past in similar circumstances.

Because of a protected characteristic

A claim for direct discrimination will only succeed if the unfavourable treatment that the pupil experienced was because of a protected characteristic. The best approach, in the majority of cases, will be to focus on the reason why, in factual terms, the responsible body acted as it did. The following principles are important:

- Motive is irrelevant.[328] There is no defence of justification to direct discrimination. It does not matter if the motive for the unfavourable treatment was to give financial assistance to a disadvantaged section of society.[329] In the employment context, an employer's decision to prevent an employee from applying for a role in the field because of their nationality, which would put the employee in genuine danger, was direct discrimination that could not be justified.[330] A genuine motive, however, is likely to be relevant to the question of remedy.

- The protected characteristic does not have to be the only reason for the treatment, or even the main reason for it, as long as it is a cause of the less favourable treatment.[331]

- It does not matter if the alleged discriminator has the same protected characteristic as the alleged victim of the discrimination.[332] A teacher who chooses boys to represent the

328 *Technical Guidance for* Schools, EHRC, paragraph 5.7

329 *James v Eastleigh Borough Council* [1990] ICR 554 HL

330 *Amnesty International v Ahmed* [2009] ICR 1450 EAT

331 *Nagarajan v London Regional Transport* [1999] ICR 877 HL

332 Equality Act 2010, section 24(1)

school in a maths competition over girls who are just as able, because they believe that boys are more authoritative or better at competitions than girls, will have committed an act of direct sex discrimination whether they are male or female.

- If the discriminator was genuinely unaware of the protected characteristic, it may be able to mount a successful defence, but it will depend on the circumstances (and note the discussion of knowledge of disability above).

Associative and perceptive discrimination[333]

Direct discrimination occurs when there is less favourable treatment because of "a" protected characteristic, rather than "his (the pupil's)" protected characteristic. This choice of language is important because it means that the person being discriminated against does not need to have the protected characteristic themselves.

Associative discrimination is discrimination based upon a pupil's association with another person who has a particular protected characteristic. For example, if a school ran an event for pupils and their parents, and excluded a particular pupil from the event because the pupil's mother had a disability that affected their behaviour, that could amount to associative discrimination.

Perceptive discrimination is discrimination based upon a perception that a pupil is a member of a relevant protected group. If a member of staff refuses to supervise a student because they believe, mistakenly, that she is a lesbian, that could amount to perceptive discrimination.

333 *Technical Guidance for Schools*, EHRC, paragraphs 5.11–12

Indirect discrimination[334]

Indirect discrimination occurs when a school applies a provision, criterion or practice ("PCP") to all pupils, or to a particular group of pupils (e.g. second-year students), but this has the effect of putting pupils (including the pupil bringing the claim) who share a particular protected characteristic within the wider group at a particular disadvantage. For a claim of indirect discrimination to succeed:

- The school applies, or would apply, the PCP equally to all relevant pupils, including pupils with a protected characteristic.

- The PCP puts, or would put, pupils sharing a protected characteristic at a particular disadvantage compared to relevant pupils who do not share that characteristic.

- The PCP puts, or would put, the particular pupil bringing the claim at that disadvantage.

- The school cannot show that the PCP is justified (i.e. that it is a proportionate means of achieving a legitimate aim).

PCPs are defined widely and can include arrangements, the way in which education or access to benefits, services or facilities are provided, one-off decisions, written or verbal policies, etc. A school's behaviour policy, and extracts from it, is a good example of a PCP, as is a uniform policy. The PCP must be non-discriminatory on its face, and applied to everyone in the same way (e.g. "no dreadlocks"). If the PCP is discriminatory on its face (e.g. "Girls may not play football"), then the claim should be for direct discrimination, or potentially harassment, depending on the circumstances.

334 *Technical Guidance for Schools,* EHRC, paragraphs 5.20–5.39

As with direct discrimination, intention and motive are irrelevant, although they may be relevant to remedy.

"Disadvantage" is not defined in the Act, but could include a loss of opportunity, or choice, or exclusion. It does not have to be capable of being financially valued. It is likely that a disadvantage has to be something that a reasonable person would complain about.

In the case of *R (Watkins-Singh) v Governing Body of Aberdare Girls' High School*[335], the claimant pupil was a Sikh who was refused permission to wear a Kara bangle, one of five external articles of faith in the Sikh religion. The Court concluded that in the context of a uniform policy, there will be a particular detriment or disadvantage if the pupil is prohibited from wearing an item when that person genuinely believed, on reasonable grounds, that wearing this item was a matter of exceptional importance to their racial identity or their religious beliefs; and the wearing of this item can be shown objectively to be of exceptional importance to their religion or race, even if the wearing of the article is not an actual requirement of that person's religion or race. In *Watkins-Singh* the school was unable to justify its uniform policy, because the Kara bangle was very small and unostentatious and therefore the prohibition on wearing the Kara bangle was not a proportionate means of achieving the legitimate aim of the uniform policy. It is important to note that *Watkins-Singh* predated the Act and therefore involved human rights considerations rather than Equality Act considerations, but the reasoning in relation to justification is similar to that required under the Equality Act and it is likely that the result would be the same.

In some cases it will be necessary to call expert evidence as to the nature of the protected characteristic involved and why a particular disadvantage arises: e.g. to establish that a behaviour policy puts a group of pupils who are disabled at a particular disadvantage.

---

335 [2008] EWHC 1865 (Admin)

George is an Afro-Caribbean boy who has never cut his hair and wears it in cornrows, as does his father and other men in his family. His school has a policy, applied to all pupils of every race and nationality, which states that hair should be clean, neat and of a moderate style. His head teacher's view is that cornrows for boys do not comply with this requirement and that they are a "gangster" hairstyle which, if permitted, risks both opening the floodgates to other outlandish hairstyles (skinheads, Mohicans) and importing gang mentality into the school. George says that his braids are a historic tradition in Africa, that they have intergenerational value and they are commonly worn by Afro-Caribbean boys and men as well as women. He refuses to remove his cornrows and is permanently excluded from the school. The High Court analyses the policy and the claimed justification of it (although not the merits of the exclusion) and concludes that the policy is not objectively justified and is therefore indirectly discriminatory on grounds of race (although not of sex).

Harassment[336]

Summary

The Act sets out 3 types of behaviour that amount to unlawful harassment. Harassment means unwanted behaviour or conduct. Note that the Act does not protect pupils against harassment by other pupils; the Act only places obligations upon responsible bodies. Schools do, however, have a duty to pupils to ensure that peer bullying which is related to a protected characteristic is taken as seriously as other forms of bullying.

---

336 Equality Act 2010, section 26; *Technical guidance for schools*, EHRC, paragraphs 5.18–5.19, 5.55–5.70

Harassment provisions only apply to disability, race and sex

It is important to note that the harassment provisions do not apply to pupils who are subjected to unwanted conduct[337] due to:

- Gender reassignment
- Religion or belief
- Sexual orientation

Where a pupil experiences unwanted conduct in relation to gender reassignment, sexual orientation or religion or belief, and as a result experiences less favourable treatment compared to people without that characteristic, it may be possible to bring that claim as direct discrimination.

Harassment related to a relevant protected characteristic

This involves:

- Unwanted behaviour
- Related to a relevant protected characteristic (limited, in the case of schools, to disability, race and sex; unwanted behaviour relating to pregnancy and maternity will almost certainly also qualify as sex-related harassment))
- Which has the purpose or effect of violating a pupil's dignity, or creating an intimidating, hostile, degrading, humiliating, or offensive environment for the pupil.

[337] Equality Act 2010, section 85(10); see *Technical guidance for schools*, EHRC, paragraphs 5.18–9

"Related to" means that the pupil does not have to have the protected characteristic himself, as with direct discrimination as discussed above: see also discussion of associative and perceptive discrimination.

Sexual harassment

This involves:

- Unwanted behaviour
- Of a sexual nature (including verbal, non-verbal or physical conduct),[338] which
- Which has the effect of violating a pupil's dignity, or creating an intimidating, hostile, degrading, humiliating or offensive environment for the pupil.

Less favourable treatment of a pupil because they submit to or reject sexual harassment related to sex

This is self-explanatory.

The purpose or effect of conduct must be to create the requisite environment

It is necessary to show that the conduct complained of had the purpose or effect of creating the requisite environment.

"Purpose" obviously involves looking at the intention of the person carrying out the conduct alleged[339] If the person's purpose is to create an intimidating, hostile, degrading, humiliating or offensive environment

338 *Technical guidance for schools*, EHRC, paragraph 5.64

339 *Technical guidance for schools*, EHRC, paragraph 5.66

for the pupil, it does not matter what the effect of the conduct was on the pupil.

> *Anna wants to be an actor, and is the only non-white member of her school's dramatic society. The teacher running the society keeps giving Anna very small or non-speaking roles, saying that unfortunately there are very few roles that are suitable for non-white actors, despite the fact that the plays chosen are silent on the ethnicity of the characters. The teacher has asked Anna to stay behind for a "little talk" three times. During these talks the teacher has told Anna that she is not really cut out for drama and should "play to her strengths" and try the dance society or choir, that she is not ladylike enough to succeed as an actor, and that she will struggle because she does not have a "traditional" name. Anna is aware that the other non-white pupils in the school who were interested in drama received similar treatment and stopped coming to the drama society after a couple of weeks. All of the other pupils have had at least one decent speaking part and none of them are asked to stay behind for "little talks". It would be possible to infer from these facts that the teacher's purpose was to create an intimidating, hostile, degrading, humiliating or offensive environment for Anna to discourage her from continuing to participate.*

If it is not possible to show purpose (and it often will be difficult to show an active intention or purpose to harass), it is enough to show that the conduct had the effect of producing the requisite environment for the pupil. In deciding whether conduct had this effect, it is necessary to consider:[340]

- The pupil's perception of the effect of the conduct (the subjective element)

340 *Technical guidance for schools*, EHRC, paragraphs 5.67–5.69

- The other circumstances of the case (for example, the personal circumstances of the pupil, any mental health issues or cultural norms or previous experiences of harassment, and the relationship between the person carrying out the harassment and the pupil or pupils experiencing the conduct)

- Whether it is reasonable for the conduct to have that effect – for example, is the pupil extremely sensitive and reading something into the conduct that is not objectively there? Would another pupil subjected to the same conduct have been offended?

Human rights considerations may also be at play where the school is a public authority (for example, a maintained school).[341] The school may need to consider whether the person accused of harassment was exercising any of their Convention rights, such as the right to freedom of thought, conscience and religion, or freedom of speech.

Victimisation

Victimisation[342] is effectively a form of whistleblowing protection that is specific to the Equality Act. If a pupil carries out what the Act terms a "protected act", it will be unlawful for the school to subject them to a detriment because they did so, or because the school believes that they did so, or because the school believes that they may do so in the future.

Detriment

A detriment means, broadly, a disadvantage,[343] even if the person imposing the detriment believes they are acting in the best interests of

341 *Technical guidance for schools*, EHRC, paragraphs 5.70

342 Equality Act 2010, section 27; see also *Technical guidance for schools*, EHRC, paragraphs 5.71–5.82

343 *Technical guidance for schools*, EHRC, paragraph 3.30–3.31 and 5.71

the pupil. It is very hard to think of circumstances in which a fixed-period exclusion or permanent exclusion would not constitute a detriment.

Protected act

A "protected act" is defined as:

- Bringing proceedings under the Act (i.e. bringing a claim for discrimination or other unlawful conduct under the Act);
- Giving evidence or information in connection with proceedings brought under the Act (for example, providing a witness statement to support another pupil's claim for discrimination against the school, or giving evidence at a hearing in support of them; note that this would also protect a pupil who gave evidence on behalf of a teacher bringing a claim for discrimination as an employee, for example);
- Doing anything else for the purposes of, or in connection with, the Act;
- Making an allegation that the school, or another person, has breached the Act (even if the allegation is later withdrawn).

Note that

- There must be a connection between the protected act and the detrimental treatment by the school.[344]
- The detrimental treatment does not need to be connected to a protected characteristic that the person making the complaint has

[344] *Technical guidance for schools*, EHRC, paragraph 5.74

- Pupils are also protected from being victimised because their parent or sibling has done a protected act.[345]

- A pupil who gives false information or evidence in bad faith is not protected against victimization.[346] However, if an original complaint is made falsely in bad faith but is supported by a pupil who genuinely believes it to be true, the supporting pupil would be protected against victimisation.[347] The fact that a complaint or claim was not upheld, however, is not sufficient of itself to prove that it was made in bad faith.

> *Marcus, a talented and ambitious actor in Year 12, is selected as one of four Year 12 Drama students to attend an external workshop hosted by a famous actor. The week before the workshop is due to take place, Marcus provides a witness statement in support of another pupil who has alleged that he was mocked by a teacher in class for being gay. The head teacher calls Marcus to his office and tells him that Marcus obviously does not care about the reputation of the school and therefore another student will attend the workshop in his place. Provided that Marcus gave his witness statement in good faith, this would constitute an act of unlawful victimisation.*

Discrimination arising from disability[348]

This occurs when a school

- Treats a disabled pupil unfavourably

345 Equality Act 2010, sections 27(1) and 86(2)

346 Equality Act 2010, section 86(3)

347 Equality Act 2010, section 86(4)

348 *Technical Guidance for Schools,* EHRC, paragraphs 5.40–5.54

- Because of something connected with their disability
- Where the unfavourable treatment cannot be justified.

Discrimination arising from disability is a category of unlawful behaviour that was created due to issues with finding a comparator in cases involving direct discrimination on the ground of disability. The problem for a disabled claimant is that often a non-disabled comparator would have received the same treatment, as this example shows:

> *Lars is frequently late for school because he has complex physical disabilities which mean that he requires support from care workers appointed by social services to get out of bed, dress, toilet and travel to school. Lars' physical needs are fluctuating and unpredictable and so his care can take as little as an hour, in which case he will be on time for school, or as long as two hours, in which case he will be late. Lars' school has a zero-tolerance policy in relation to punctuality and he regularly receives detention because he is late so often. Henrik, a non-disabled student, is frequently late for school because he is an avid reader and frequently loses track of time. He is late as often as Lars and receives a similar number of detentions. Lars cannot bring a direct discrimination claim because he cannot show that he has been treated less favourably than a non-disabled comparator.*

Unfavourable treatment

Discrimination arising from disability replaces the requirement of less favourable treatment plus comparator with a requirement to show "unfavourable treatment"[349]. Unfavourable treatment means that the disabled pupil has been put at a disadvantage. It is very hard to imagine circumstances in which a decision to exclude a child from school would not constitute unfavourable treatment. In fact, all disciplinary sanctions

349 *Technical guidance for schools*, EHRC, paragraphs 5.44–47

are likely to constitute unfavourable treatment; they are intended to be unfavourable; that is how sanctions work. This does not mean that a child with a disability can never be given a sanction, but it does mean that teachers must be on the lookout for situations in which a child's misconduct is related to their disability, and ensure that any unfavourable treatment is objectively justified.

Unfavourable treatment is not enough of itself to establish a claim for discrimination arising from disability, but it is a necessary element.

Arising from the pupil's disability

The unfavourable treatment must be because of something that has arisen as a consequence of the pupil's disability. What this means will vary from case to case depending upon the nature and effect of the disability upon the pupil. For example, a pupil's disability may mean that they have disturbed sleep, which in turn may make it difficult for them to get to school on time, or that they have difficulty controlling their behaviour (perhaps due to anxiety or sensory processing issues), so are more likely to breach the school's behaviour policy.

> *Dana has ADHD, which makes it hard for her to focus for long periods of time in class. As her ability to attend wanes, Dana becomes lively and boisterous, talking whilst the teacher is talking and distracting other pupils instead of getting on with her work; she may also become rude and argumentative when teachers attempt to intervene. Dana receives regular warnings and detentions, which constitute unfavourable treatment because of something that arises as a consequence of Dana's disability.*

Justification defence

If there is unfavourable treatment of a pupil arising from their disability, the school will have a defence to the claim if it is able to justify the treatment (unlike direct discrimination, which cannot be justified),[350] Unfavourable treatment will be justified if it is, objectively viewed,

- a proportionate means
- of achieving a legitimate aim.

The burden of justifying the treatment is upon the school, and a defence of justification must be based upon evidence rather than stereotypes or assumptions.

> *Margo has generalised anxiety disorder. She is under the care of CAMHS. Margo's school offers a trip to the Danish Christmas markets every winter; Margo's friends are going and she would like to go too. However, the SENCo refuses to accept the deposit from her parents, telling them that it is obvious that Margo would not be able to cope away from home for four days, and the school cannot accept the responsibility of taking her. She does not ask them if Margo has spent time away from home before, canvass any suggestions for strategies to help Margo cope, or take measures to consult with CAMHS or Nitin's GP. Safeguarding Margo's peers and staff is likely to be a legitimate aim. However, since this decision is based on the SENCo's assumptions around Margo's condition rather than an evidence-based risk assessment specific to Margo and the proposed activity, it would be hard to justify.*

Legitimate aims will vary depending upon the situation, but common aims cited in exclusion cases include

- Upholding and maintaining appropriate standards of behaviour in the school

350 *Technical guidance for schools*, EHRC, paragraph 5.32, 5.48–49

- Safeguarding the school's external reputation

- Safeguarding other staff and pupils at school

"Proportionate" means that there was no reasonable step that the school could have taken, short of the action that constitutes the unfavourable treatment, to achieve the legitimate aim. There is, therefore, a strong cross-over with the duty upon schools to make reasonable adjustments, considered elsewhere in this chapter.[351] Schools must identify any reasonable adjustments that can be made for disabled pupils promptly, and consistent in their monitoring and review of any reasonable adjustments already in place. Reasonable adjustments should also be fully reviewed and considered by the head teacher when considering whether or not to exclude – both those currently in place, and any that might be put in place. If, following a decision to exclude, it transpires that there were reasonable adjustments that could have been made that could have avoided the exclusion (assuming that this was or should have been obvious to the head teacher on the information available at the time), then the school may not be able to justify the unfavourable treatment.

For example, parents may argue that the school could have:

- Sought additional or updated advice from appropriate agencies and clinicians (e.g. where a disabled pupil was identified as being at risk of exclusion, or at the point where the decision to exclude was being considered by the head teacher)

- Consulted the pupil's Local Authority

- Made adjustments to policies, for example the behaviour policy (e.g. to provide for more informal warnings before a formal warning is imposed, or more formal warnings before a detention

351 *Technical guidance for schools*, EHRC, paragraph 5.53–54 and further case law.

is imposed, etc) or uniform policy (to avoid subjecting a pupil with sensory issues to disciplinary sanctions for not being able to tolerate particular items of clothing)

- Put in place other strategies, e.g. a "yellow card" permitting a pupil with behavioural or sensory issues to choose to leave the classroom and go to a pre-agreed quiet room or safe place when they feel themselves becoming anxious or dysregulated.

This is obviously not an exhaustive list, since the adjustments that can reasonably be made will always vary depending upon individual circumstances.

Ella has anxiety issues and sensory processing difficulties which led to periodic outbursts in her classroom. An independently commissioned Occupational Therapy report advised that Ella required 1:1 weekly sessions from an Occupational Therapist throughout the year, and that she should have access to a Quiet Room whenever she started to become dysregulated. The school supported Ella's parents in an application for an EHC Needs Assessment to obtain the OT for Ella, but did not inform all of her teachers that she must be permitted to go to the Quiet Room if she was becoming dysregulated. Most teachers did permit Ella to leave when she asked; one teacher attempted to discipline Ella when she tried to leave the classroom, which resulted in the classroom having to be evacuated as Ella screamed and threw chairs across the room. The Tribunal might or might not accept that the school could not reasonably be expected to fund the Occupational Therapy itself without an EHC Plan in place (depending upon the circumstances and resources available to the school and steps taken by it). However, a decision to exclude would be difficult to justify if the Tribunal was satisfied that Ella's outburst could have been avoided by using the quiet room strategy suggested by the OT.

Knowledge defence

If a school can show that it neither knew, nor could reasonably be expected to know, that the pupil is suffering from a disability, then that would also be a complete defence to a claim for discrimination arising from disability, as discussed above.[352]

In *SS v Proprietory of an Independent School* [2024] UKUT 29 (AAC), the Upper Tribunal gave the following guidance on claims for discrimination arising from disability. There are five questions to be asked:

- Whether the disabled person has been treated unfavourably; note that the refusal of a "treat" such as (in this case) an extra session with a therapy dog is capable of amounting to unfavourable treatment in principle, but may not in the circumstances of a particular case. Note also that at this stage the only question is whether there is unfavourable treatment; the question of whether any such treatment is linked to disability arises later.

- The conscious or unconscious reason for the unfavourable treatment. For example, in *SS*, if a treat had been withheld as a sanction for a child's violence and aggression, then the reason would be the child's violence and aggression. Note that the reason does not need to be the only or sole reason, just a more than minor or trivial influence on the unfavourable treatment.

- Whether that reason is something arising in consequence of the disabled person's disability; this is an objective question, which does not involve consideration of the mental processes of the

352 *Technical guidance for schools*, EHRC, paragraph 5.50–51. See also *The University of Bristol v (1) Dr Robert Abrahart (administrator of the estate of Natasha Abrahart, deceased), (2) the EHRC* [2024] EWHC 299 (KB) which includes a detailed analysis of the legal framework around knowledge of disability, whether actual or constructive.

alleged discriminator; this is where the question of a link to the claimant's disability comes in);

- Whether the school new, or could reasonably have been expected to know, that the person had the disability relied on;

- If so, whether the school has shown that the treatment is a proportionate means of achieving a legitimate aim.

Duty to make reasonable adjustments[353]

It is important to note that by Schedule 13 (4) of the Act, a decision to exclude cannot itself constitute a failure to make reasonable adjustments. As set out above, however, if a school has failed to make reasonable adjustments for a disabled pupil, or fails to appreciate that there are reasonable adjustments that can be made that would remove the need to exclude, then that would be relevant to a claim for disability arising from discrimination. This is because if there were reasonable adjustments that could have been made and could be made going forward that would avoid the need for a fixed-term or permanent exclusion, then the responsible body may struggle to justify the decision to exclude.

The duty to make reasonable steps for responsible bodies is a duty to:

- take such steps as it is reasonable to take

- to avoid a substantial disadvantage to a disabled person

- which is caused by

    - a provision, criterion or practice ("PCP") applied by or on behalf of a responsible body, which

353 *Technical Guidance for Schools*, EHRC, chapter 6

        - puts disabled pupils generally at a substantial disadvantage in relation to provision of education or access to a benefit, facility or service,

        - in comparison with persons who are not disabled,[354] or

    - the absence of an auxiliary aid or service.

Accordingly, parents of children with disabilities and disabled young people, when bringing claims for failure to make reasonable adjustments, will need to show the following:

- that the PCP disadvantages a particular group of disabled pupils, including their own child; and

- that it does not so impact persons who do not have that disability.[355]

Accordingly, when bringing a claim for failure to make reasonable adjustments against a Responsible Body, the FtT must compare the impact of the PCP on a particular group of pupils with a particular disability, with the impact (or otherwise) on a group of non-disabled persons (or persons who do not share that disability). This will sometimes

---

354 Note that the reasonable adjustments duty under section 20(3) is modified in its application to responsible bodies of schools by schedule 13, paragraph 2 of the Equality Act: cases from the employment sphere should be treated with some caution when considered in the education context.

355 A Multi-Academy Trust v RR [2024] UKUT 9 (AAC). Note that this case involved a special school, and also clarified that even if all children in a special school share the same disability, the impact of the PCP upon them can be compared to what its impact would be against a hypothetical group of non-disabled persons (i.e. the claim does not necessarily fail just because all children in a school share a disability).

be straightforward – for example, where there is a PCP that handouts are to be printed in 12-point font, it may be easy to show that children with particular visual impairments will be adversely affected by this compared to persons who do not have that impairment. In other cases, the comparison may be more complicated (e.g. establishing that a PCP impacts children with ADHD, where symptoms can vary and evidence can be unclear; this may require parents and young people to obtain expert evidence, which is expensive and time-consuming.)

Some readers may be aware that in the employment context there is also a duty to make adjustments to physical features of the workplace. This does not apply to schools in relation to disabled pupils; they have, instead, a general duty to plan better access for disabled pupils, including in relation to the school's physical environment.

The duty is anticipatory, meaning that schools must consider in advance what disabled pupils might require and what adjustments they should make.

Note that schools are permitted to exercise their professional opinions to try particular strategies for a period of time before making adjustments, or to allow time for reflection and assessment before deciding to make changes – in other words, the fact that a strategy that the school adopts does not work for a child immediately does not necessarily mean that the school is breaking the law by continuing to attempt the strategy for a period of time before adjusting. Furthermore, there is no duty to achieve a goal or objective under the duty to make reasonable adjustments.[356]

Lastly, schools are not entitled, under any circumstances, to charge pupils or parents for reasonable adjustments. Reasonable adjustments are to be funded by the school.

---

356 *KTS v Governing Body of a Primary School* [2024] UKUT 139 AAC

Provision, criterion or practice ("PCP")

There is no definition of this term in the Act, but the phrase is generally considered to cover written policies, practices (whether written down or just generally understood) and decisions taken by the school. Behaviour policies and uniform policies are both PCPs. A decision taken in relation to a group of children (e.g. that second year students will not be allowed to go into a particular part of the school at a particular time) will constitute a PCP. The essential point about a PCP is that, as with indirect discrimination, it must be neutral on its face.

> *St Kylie's School for Young Ladies has a uniform policy which requires all pupils to wear a particular brand of black shoe. The policy stipulates that any pupil caught without their boater will receive an immediate detention. Lisa has a diagnosis of ASD and is unable to tolerate the material that the shoe is made of, but her mother has located a very similar-looking shoe that is made of material that Lisa can tolerate. It would be a reasonable adjustment for St Kylie's to allow Lisa to wear the alternative shoe.*

Substantial disadvantage

The PCP must be neutrally expressed and applied, but must put the disabled pupil at a substantial disadvantage. "Substantial" means more than minor or trivial, and is to be judged in light of the individual circumstances. This could cover anything from a student with an impairment which means that they can only read documents prepared in a particular way or with particular auxiliary aids, to pupils with conditions that affect their concentration or behaviour across the day.

Reasonable steps

The Act does not define "reasonable". Nor is there a specific defence of justification. There is an implied defence in the sense that schools do not have to make adjustments that are not reasonable. The factors to be taken into account are:

- The extent to which special educational provision will be provided to the disabled pupil under Part 3 of the Children and Families Act 2014 (i.e. an EHC Plan)
- The resources of the school and the availability of financial or other assistance (e.g. funding from the Local Authority or other agencies)
- The financial and other costs of making the adjustments
- The extent to which taking a step would be effective in overcoming the substantial disadvantage
- The practicability of the adjustment
- The effect of the disability on the pupil
- Health and safety concerns
- Maintaining academic, musical, sporting and other standards
- Interests of other pupils and prospective pupils.

Pregnancy and maternity discrimination

Schools must not discriminate against pupils because of pregnancy or maternity, or because they are breastfeeding.[357] This means that the school cannot withdraw or limit the education or facilities or other benefits that it offers to pupils from a pupil for this reason. However, a

---

357 Equality Act 2010, section 17; *Technical guidance for schools*, EHRC, paragraph 3.32, 5.14–5.16

school can offer additional benefits to pregnant or breastfeeding pupils, or provide them in a more flexible or favourable way than they are offered to other pupils.

> *Claire has always achieved very high marks at school, but accidentally became pregnant at 15. She has decided that she wants to keep the baby. Claire's Maths teacher tells her that she will not be able to do Maths A-level because she won't have enough time for it now that she has decided to have a baby. When Claire is obviously upset by this, the teacher is surprised and says that she didn't think Claire would be interested now anyway. This is likely to constitute pregnancy and maternity discrimination.*

> *Marcy has returned to school after the birth of her baby, who is looked after during the day by her parents. She lives ten minutes' walk from the school. Students are not allowed to leave school premises at lunchtime. However, after discussion with the school it is agreed that Marcy should be allowed to go home for lunch so that she can feed her baby at the same time.*

It is important to remember that the treatment required to prove direct discrimination due to pregnancy or maternity is *unfavourable* treatment, not *less favourable* treatment: in other words, there is no need for a comparator in pregnancy/maternity cases (see discussion of comparators in direct discrimination, above).

Prohibited conduct relating to schools

Part 6 of the Act sets out the circumstances in which it will be unlawful for education providers (schools, further education providers and higher education institutions) to discriminate against those to whom they provide education based on a protected characteristic. For our purposes the relevant part is Chapter 1 of Part 6, which sets out the duties of the responsible body of a school:

- It must not discriminate against[358] or victimise[359] prospective pupils in relation to admissions arrangements, offers or refusals to admit. This could be relevant to arrangements in relation to managed moves.

- It must not discriminate against[360] or victimise[361] a pupil in the way it provides education to them; affords them access to a benefit, facility or service; by not providing education to the pupil or by not affording them access to a benefit, facility or service; by excluding the pupil from the school; or by subjecting the pupil to any other detriment.

- It must not harass a pupil or prospective pupil.[362]

- It has a duty to make reasonable adjustments in relation to disabled pupils at the school.[363]

These provisions are deliberately widely drawn. They mean that a school must not discriminate in relation to provision of formal education, to extracurricular / "enrichment" activities, taking place after school, outside of school (e.g. school trips), or during breaks or lunches, as well

358 Equality Act 2010, section 85(1)

359 Equality Act 2010, section 85(4)

360 Equality Act 2010, section 85(2)

361 Equality Act 2010, section 85(5)

362 Equality Act 2010, section 85(3)

363 Equality Act 2010, section 85(6)

as the use of school facilities. The EHRC advises that the following must be discrimination-free:[364]

- Policies and procedures (including behaviour or discipline policies, uniform policies or dress codes, etc). Behaviour or disciplinary policies in particular must allow for a certain amount of flexibility. Some children with conditions such as ADHD, autism or PDA will be much more likely to break school rules. Schools are strongly advised to make it clear within the behaviour policy itself that the policy may be adjusted for disabled pupils, and to retain contemporaneous records of decisions made in relation to reasonable adjustments. Schools must also ensure that all forms of bullying by pupils, whether related to a racial characteristic or not, are taken equally seriously and attract the same sanctions (e.g. it would be potentially directly discriminatory for religion-related bullying to attract a warning but for race-related bullying to attract a suspension).

- The way in which the curriculum is delivered, on and off site. Note that this does not include the curriculum itself.[365] For example, it is lawful to teach using provocative materials, such as showing pupils of appropriate age *The Last Temptation of Christ.* It is also permissible to teach evolution even if doing so offends against some pupils' religious beliefs.

- School trips

- Arrangements for tests and examinations

- Academic and vocational options

---

364 *Technical guidance for schools*, EHRC, paragraphs 3.3–3.20

365 *Technical guidance for schools*, EHRC, paragraph 3.22–3.23

- Provision of information and advice relating to careers

- Work experience and work placements (insofar as allocation to work placements is concerned; a school will not normally be responsible for discrimination occurring whilst a pupil is on work experience).

- After school clubs, leisure and sports

- School facilities (library, labs, IT, dining halls, playgrounds, sports facilities)

Statutory exceptions to the prohibition on direct discrimination in schools

Acts of collective worship,[366] schools with a religious character or ethos,[367] and single-sex schools[368] are permissible via specific statutory exceptions to the prohibition on direct discrimination.

Duties under the Act owed by schools to former pupils

Ex-pupils of a school are also protected from discrimination, harassment and victimisation, provided that the unlawful conduct arises out of and is closely connected with the pupil's previous relationship with the school, and would have been unlawful if they were still a pupil. This includes a duty to make reasonable adjustments for former disabled pupils, if the substantial disadvantage arises out of and is closely connected with the person's having been a pupil.

366 Equality Act 2010, schedule 11, paragraph 6

367 Equality Act 2010, schedule 11, paragraph 5

368 Equality Act 2010, schedule 11, paragraphs 1 and 2

> *A school invites alumni to a lecture followed by afternoon tea in a part of the school that is only accessible by steps. A former pupil who is now a wheelchair user asks if the location can be changed to enable him to attend as well. Whether or not this was a reasonable adjustment would depend upon all of the circumstances as well as the resources and facilities available to the school, but the school could not refuse to make the adjustment because it was requested by someone who is no longer a pupil.*

Liability of Responsible Bodies for acts of employees and agents

Responsible Bodies are liable for contraventions of the Act that are carried out by their employees in the course of their employment, regardless of whether or not they knew or approved of the thing that was done.[369] Such acts will be treated as having been done by the employer.[370] This means, for example, that a claim may be brought against a Responsible Body for discriminatory conduct by an individual teacher in respect of a pupil during a lesson.

Responsible Bodies are also liable for the acts of their agents,[371] provided the agent was exercising the authority of the Responsible Body, regardless of whether the Responsible Body knew or approved of the thing that was done;[372] it is not necessary to show that the Responsible Body authorised the agent to discriminate.[373] Common-law principles of principal-agency liability apply.[374]

[369] Equality Act 2010, section 109(3)

[370] Equality Act 2010, section 109(1)

[371] Equality Act 2010, section 109(2)

[372] Equality Act 2010, section 109(3)

[373] *Bungay and another v Saini and others* EAT 0331/10

[374] *Unite the Union v Nailard* [2019] ICR 28 CA

"Reasonable steps" defence

The Responsible Body may be able to avoid liability for the acts of its employees if it is able to show that, prior to the discriminatory act,[375] it took all reasonable steps to prevent the employee either from doing the act that was done, or from doing anything of that description.[376] Reasonable steps generally involves ensuring that appropriate equal opportunities policies are in place, that they are reviewed regularly and that suitable training is provided to employees.[377] It is for the Responsible Body to establish that reasonable steps were taken. In the employment context it has been held that the Tribunal should take the following approach when deciding whether the defence is made out:

- Ask whether there were any preventative steps taken by the employer; and

- Ask whether there were any further preventative steps that the employer could have taken, that were reasonably practicable.[378]

Personal liability of employees and agents

The individual employee or agent may also be personally liable for the contravention of the Act[379] if:

- The individual is an employee or agent of the Responsible Body

---

375 See *Mahood v Irish Centre Housing Ltd* EAT 0228/10; it is not enough to show that the discrimination was rectified after the event.

376 Equality Act 2010, section 109(4)

377 *Technical Guidance for Schools*, EHRC, paragraphs 5.87 and 5.88

378 *Canniffe v East Riding of Yorkshire Council* [2000] IRLR 555 EAT

379 Equality Act 2010, section 110(1)

- They did something that is treated as having been done by the Responsible Body under section 109(1) or (2); and

- Doing that thing amounts to a contravention of the Act by the employer

This means that where a teacher discriminates against a pupil in the classroom, both the Responsible Body and the individual teacher may be liable under the Act. The only exception to this is where the discriminatory act is an act of disability discrimination. In those circumstances only the Responsible Body may be sued.[380]

In most cases the individual's defence is likely to focus on the facts. It is also a defence, however, for the individual to show that they relied upon a statement by the Responsible Body that the act that they did was not a contravention of the Act, and that it was reasonable for them to so rely.[381] Responsible Bodies should note that it is a criminal offence under the Act to knowingly or recklessly make a statement to an employee or principal that is false or misleading in a material respect.[382]

There is an important exception in the schools context here, which is that employees of Responsible Bodies cannot be personally sued for acts of disability discrimination.

Instructing, causing and inducing discrimination

The Act makes it unlawful for a person to instruct, cause or induce someone to discriminate, harass or victimise another person, regardless of whether the person who is instructed to do so carries out the instruction.[383] This applies to all forms of prohibited conduct in the

---

380 Equality Act 2010, section 110(7)

381 Equality Act 2010, section 110(3)

382 Equality Act 2010, section 110(4) and (5)

383 Equality Act 2010, section 111(1)–(3)

schools context under Part 6 Chapter 1. Inducement may be direct or indirect.[384] In order to give rise to a claim, the person giving the instruction and the person being instructed must be in a legal relationship which is itself regulated by the Equality Act (for example, an employment relationship).[385]

Claims may be brought under this section by the person who was given the instruction, if they suffered a detriment; by any third party (for example, a pupil) who suffered a detriment as a result of the giving of the instruction, causation or inducement of discrimination; or by the EHRC.[386]

The Act makes it unlawful for a person to knowingly help another to do anything which amounts to a contravention under the Act, including all forms of prohibited conduct in the schools context under Part 6 Chapter 1[387] *apart* from disability discrimination.[388] Again, it is a defence for the person giving the help to show that they relied upon a statement by the Responsible Body that the act that they did was not a contravention of the Act, and that it was reasonable for them to so rely,[389] and a criminal offence to provide such a statement knowing or being reckless as to whether it was false or misleading in a material respect.[390]

---

384 Equality Act 2010, section 111(4)

385 Equality Act 2010, section 111(7)

386 Equality Act 2010, section 111(5)

387 Equality Act 2010, section 112

388 Equality Act 2010, section 112(6)

389 Equality Act 2010, section 112(2)

390 Equality Act 2010, section 112(3)

Where parents wish to bring a claim under the Equality Act and also seek a review before the Independent Review Panel

See "Where parents' case includes allegations of discrimination" in Chapter 3.

Bringing a claim for discrimination under the Act

Claims under the Equality Act 2010 can be complex, and there can be costs consequences if a claim or a defence is unsuccessful (especially in the County Court, although the extent of the risk depends upon the value and complexity of the claim). Whilst the First-tier Tribunal is generally costs neutral (i.e. there are only limited circumstances in which a party will be ordered to pay some or all of another party's costs), and considerably less formal and more accessible, presenting and defending discrimination claims in that forum can still be complicated. Accordingly, we strongly recommend that parents contemplating a discrimination claim, and schools who are aware that such a claim is likely to be brought, seek legal advice as to the merits of any discrimination claim and (particularly in the County Court) the extent of any costs exposure.

Parents may wish to try to resolve things informally with the school prior to presenting a claim. This is not unreasonable. All schools, independent and maintained, will have a complaints procedure which allows parents to present complaints to the governors or trustees to see if they can be resolved. The important thing to bear in mind is that there are strict time limits in place for bringing claims for discrimination under the Act, as set out below, which are extremely difficult to extend and so must be adhered to even if the complaints process has not yet come to an end.

Parents may also wish to ensure that they have all of the information that they require relating their child's time at the school. This can be done either via pre-action correspondence, or – possibly more effectively – by making a Subject Access Request under the GDPR requiring the school to provide copies of all documentation relating to the pupil (subject to certain defined excepted categories of information). Numerous templates for doing so can be found online. Again, there are strict time limits under the GDPR with which schools must comply, but a deadline for bringing a claim for discrimination under the Act must be met even if the school has not yet responded, as the deadlines are strict and it is very difficult to obtain an extension of them.

Freedom of Information Act (FOIA) requests may also be made to schools. These requests cover information that is not specific or personal to the pupil (or to other pupils) but which may be of use in a discrimination claim, such as anonymised information regarding the school's disability practices and policies. Again, if information has not been received under an FOIA request and the deadline for presenting a claim for discrimination is approaching, the deadline for presenting the claim must be met even if the FOIA information has not been received.

Venue and time limits

The County Court

Overview

All claims for discrimination are brought in the County Court, save for disability discrimination claims against schools by pupils, which must be brought in the First-tier Tribunal. In the County Court, the claim must be made in the pupil's name. If the pupil lacks mental capacity, or is under school leaving age, they must make the claim through a "litigation friend". This is an adult (usually, but not always, a parent) who is appointed to conduct the claim on their behalf.

The County Court is a civil court. It considers a wide range of types of claim, ranging from lower value small claims to fast track and multi-track cases worth thousands of pounds. It operates a formal procedure, although litigants in person do regularly appear before it, particularly in lower-value claims.

Costs

The County Court is a civil court and so there is potentially a costs risk in terms of bringing a discrimination claim before it, particularly if the claim is assigned to the fast-track or multi-track rather than the small claims track. A full discussion in relation to costs is beyond the scope of this book, but the starting point on costs is that the party that has succeeded is entitled to have its reasonable legal costs paid by the other side. It is important for anyone contemplating a claim in the County Court to fully understand the merits and likely value of their own claim, and the costs risk involved in doing so if the claim does not succeed.

Equality Act assessors

Unlike the First-tier Tribunal, discrimination claims in the County Court are not heard by specialists in education, SEN or discrimination. For this reason, the County Court is able to appoint an Equality Act assessor when it hears discrimination claims,[391] to assist the judge. Generally speaking, a County Court judge must appoint an assessor in a claim under the Equality Act 2010, unless there is a good reason not to do so.

Time limits in the County Court

A claim in the County Court must be brought within 6 months of the date of the act or omission complained of.[392] If what is complained of is discriminatory conduct extending over a period, time will start running

391 County Courts Act 1984, section 63; rule 35.15 CPR. See also Cary v Commissioner of Police for the Metropolis [2014] EWCA Civ 987 which confirmed that an assessor need not be specialist in the area of discrimination (here sexuality).

392 Equality Act 2010, section 118(1)(a)

at the end of that period. Failure to do something is to be treated as occurring when the person in question decided on it.[393] If there is no evidence as to when the decision not to do something was made, then it will be taken to have been made on the date when the person making the decision does an act inconsistent with doing it, or the end of the period when the person might reasonably have been expected to do it.[394] It can sometimes be difficult to know when the deadline for bringing a claim is in a case that goes back over an extended period of time and involves a number of discriminatory acts and omissions, in which case it is sensible to take legal advice as early as possible.

There is a limited jurisdiction to extend time for such period as the County Court thinks just and equitable[395] but extensions of time are very difficult to obtain in practice and cannot be guaranteed if the deadline is not met.

The First-tier Tribunal

Overview

Equality Act claims against schools – including independent schools – are to be brought in the County Court, *unless* the claim in question is a disability discrimination claim against a school (again including independent schools), in which case it must be brought in the First-tier Tribunal (Health, Education and Social Care Chamber).[396]

---

393 Equality Act 2010, section 118(6)

394 Equality Act 2010, section 118(7)

395 Equality Act 2010, section 118(1)(b)

396 Equality Act 2010, section 114, section 116(1), Schedule 17 Part 2

A discrimination claim in the First Tier Tribunal can be brought either by a person with parental responsibility for a child or young person, or a young person who is over compulsory school age.[397]

Costs

In the First-tier Tribunal, the general rule is that each side pays its own costs, and neither side pays or contributes to the other side's costs. The First-tier Tribunal has the power to make costs orders only where it considers that a party or its representative has acted unreasonably in bringing, defending or conducting the proceedings.[398] However, it does not have to do so even where unreasonable conduct is established. In practice, this power tends to be exercised rarely, although costs orders are not unheard of. For this reason, the costs risk of bringing a claim in the First-tier Tribunal is considerably lower than in the County Court.

No assessor required

The First-tier Tribunal is a specialist tribunal in the area of education, special educational needs and disability. Assessors do not sit with the Tribunal as they do in the County Court.

Time limits in the First-tier Tribunal

Time limits are set out in Schedule 17, Part 4 of the Act. The provisions for time limits are the same as for the County Court, save that there is no reference to a "just and equitable" extension of time; the Schedule states only that the Tribunal "*may consider a claim which is out of time*".[399] The Schedule also provides that where the contravention is attributable to a

---

397 Equality Act 2010, Schedule 17, paragraph 3

398 First-tier Tribunal (Health, Education and Social Care Chamber) Rules, Consolidated version as at 13th November 2019, rule 10(1)(b)

399 Equality Act 2010, Schedule 17(4)(3)

term in a contract, the conduct is to be treated as extending throughout the duration of the contract.[400]

It is important to be clear about when continuing acts start and when they end, and about the difference between acts and omissions. For example, in *Governing Body of School T v AA and RA* [2023] UKUT 311 (AAC), the FTT's finding (in favour of the parents) that there had been a continuing relationship with the school until 11 May 2021 (which meant that the claim had been brought in time) was overturned by the Upper Tribunal because the child had in fact moved out of commutable distance to the school a month before after which the school was no longer responsible for any element of his education; accordingly no discriminatory acts could have taken place beyond that point.

Record-keeping and evidence in discrimination claims

We have looked elsewhere (for example, in Chapter 2) at the type of records that schools can reasonably be expected to keep. These are relevant in any subsequent proceedings, whether before the governing board, the Independent Review Panel, the First-tier Tribunal, the County Court or the Administrative Court. All of that information will be relevant and important in a discrimination claim. The school will be expected to produce evidence relating to:

- The pupil's behaviour (e.g. behaviour log)
- Information relating to the pupil's disability, e.g. expert reports or medication information shared with the school, any referrals by the school to external services and the results of such referrals

[400] Equality Act 2010, Schedule 17(5)(a)

- Evidence of any correspondence with the Local Authority regarding the pupil's SEN or suspected SEN (e.g. applications for EHC Needs Assessments or for high needs block funding)

- Reasonable adjustments agreed upon with the pupil/parents, including to the behaviour policy (e.g. more warnings, avoiding a particular sanction or detentions etc to be carried out in a quiet room/with a particular teacher) and evidence that these reasonable adjustments were shared with the staff working with the pupil

- Evidence that any EHC Plan has been shared with the staff working with the pupil and that any provision (e.g. speech and language therapy, social skills group) has been provided

- Evidence that any training required in relation to the pupil, pursuant to an EHC Plan, expert advice shared with the school and/or in relation to reasonable adjustments agreed has been given to staff working with the pupil

Parents may keep some records themselves – for example, emails sent to and received from staff at the school – but parents are not in the classroom with their children at school. The school is likely to be seen by the Independent Review Panel, First-tier Tribunal and County Court as being in the best position to record matters relevant to the pupil. Any failure to keep appropriate records, or adequate records, of matters relevant to the pupil's progress, behaviours and disability or learning difficulties is likely to attract criticism at best and, at worst, result in a reversal of the burden of proof (see below).

Burden and standard of proof in Equality Act claims

This is a general summary of how the burden and standard of proof operates under the Equality Act. The precise considerations will vary depending on the form of discrimination or unlawful conduct alleged. Further information can be found in the sections on specific forms of discrimination set out earlier in the chapter.

In order to decide whether or not there has been a contravention of the Act, the court or tribunal must start by finding facts – that is, deciding what actually happened. Only once the facts have been found can the court apply the law to them and decide whether unlawful conduct took place. In civil proceedings the usual rule is that the person who brings the case (the claimant) has to prove their case on the balance of probabilities (i.e. that it is more likely than not that what they say happened, happened).

Under the Act, the burden of proof works differently, and is slightly more favourable to claimants. This is because the courts have241recognised that discrimination is often not obvious and can be difficult to prove. Broadly, the parent/claimant is required to show that there are facts from which the court could decide, in the absence of any other explanation, that the school committed an unlawful act of discrimination, harassment or victimisation under the Act (i.e. establishing a prima facie case).[401] If they are able to do so, the burden of proof shifts to the school. The school must then prove that it did not commit the act, or that there is a non-discriminatory explanation for whatever happened. If it is unable to do so, it will lose.

Generally speaking, to establish a prima facie case a claimant will need to point to something from which an inference of discrimination can be made; it is not enough simply to point to less favourable treatment and a difference in race, religion, gender, etc. However, the something more

---

401 Equality Act 2010, section 136; see also *Efobi v Royal Mail Group Ltd* [2019] ICR 750 CA

need not be a great deal; it might be an inference drawn from an evasive or untruthful answer, or a failure to respond at all.[402]

Remedies

In the County Court

The County Court has the power to award all of the remedies available to the High Court on a claim for tort (negligence) or a claim for judicial review. These include:

- A declaration that unlawful conduct has taken place under the Act (or that no such conduct has taken place). A declaration on its own does not require any person to do anything or prevent them from doing something, but it is a binding and (unless successfully appealed) conclusive declaration of the lawfulness or unlawfulness of the school's conduct.

- An injunction requiring the school to do something, or to prevent the school from doing something (e.g. repeating a discriminatory act). There is as yet no authority confirming that the County Court can make an order for reinstatement of a pupil, although the First-tier Tribunal can.

- Damages to compensate for any loss suffered by the person bringing the claim, and interest on any compensation awarded. This includes both specific financial loss (e.g. having to purchase new uniform or school supplies) and compensation for injury to feelings. Injury to feelings is compensation for the injury to feelings caused by the discriminatory act. Such awards are known

---

402 *Deman v Commission for Equality and Human Rights and ors* [2010] EWCA Civ 1279 CA

as "*Vento* awards" and fall into three value bands[403] depending on the seriousness of the conduct and its effect upon the individual:

- £1,200–£11,700 for lower band offences: these are cases involving one-off or minor incidents of discrimination, such as a single discriminatory insult.
- £11,700–£35,200 for middle band offences. These are cases which are serious, including for example a serious one-off incident of discrimination, but where an award in the upper band is not appropriate
- £35,200–£58,700 for upper band offences. These are reserved for the most serious offences, such as a discriminatory campaign which had a profound impact upon the victim (e.g. depression, anxiety, or extreme distress).

- Vento awards are entirely discriminatory, although it would be unusual for no award to be made at all where discrimination was found. Judges have considerable discrimination both in choosing the appropriate band for award, and in deciding what amount within the band is appropriate. Most of the authorities in relation to *Vento* awards derive from employment cases, so are not necessarily very well translated to cases involving pupils at school; but what is clear is that relevant factors include the seriousness of the incident, whether it was a one-off incident or a campaign; the motivation behind the incident (well-meaning intention gone wrong or malicious/indifferent as to impact); and the impact upon the victim.

---

403 As of 6th April 2024; they are periodically revised to take account of inflation

- Costs orders (see discussion above).

In the First-tier Tribunal

The First-tier Tribunal can make any order that it thinks appropriate in the individual case, including an order for reinstatement of an excluded child.[404] However, it cannot order the payment of any compensation. It follows that victims of disability discrimination who are pupils at school cannot claim *Vento* awards or compensation for specific financial losses.

In cases where the discrimination constitutes a breach of contract, or educational negligence, it may be possible to bring a claim for breach of contract or negligence in the County Court, relying upon the First-tier Tribunal's finding that the school discriminated against the pupil; but this is a complicated sort of claim to bring, and so we would strongly advise any parent considering such a course of action to seek legal advice first.

Note that in a claim for breach of contract or educational negligence the County Court would have no power to order a *Vento* award, and so financial recovery would be likely to be limited to specific financial losses.

Examples of orders that the First-tier Tribunal can make include:

- Reinstatement of a pupil who has been excluded (but note that the First-tier Tribunal does not have to order reinstatement, even if it considers that an exclusion was discriminatory, and may be particularly reluctant to do so if it is clear that the relationship between school and pupil has irretrievably broken down)

- A requirement to provide additional education to the pupil to make up for the education missed

---

404 *Proprietor of Ashdown House School v (1) JKL (2) MNP* [2019] UKUT 259 (AAC)

- Requiring the school to write a letter of apology
- Ordering the school to provide training to staff (e.g. training from the National Autism Society or other relevant charity)
- Requiring the school to redraft policies or procedures that have been found to be discriminatory

Public Sector Equality Duty[405]

The Public Sector Equality Duty (PSED) is a duty upon public bodies to promote equality. There are two aspects of the duty:

- The general equality duty, which is for schools to have due regard, in carrying out their functions, to the need to[406]
    - Eliminate discrimination, harassment, victimisation and other unlawful discriminatory conduct;
    - Advance equality of opportunity between people who share a protected characteristic and people who do not, by having due regard to the need to
        - Remove or minimise disadvantages
        - Take steps to meet different needs
        - Encourage participation when it is disproportionately low

405 *Public Sector Equality Duty Guidance for Schools in England*, EHRC

406 Equality Act 2010, section 149(1)

- Foster good relations across all protected characteristics, between people who share a protected characteristic and people who do not.

- The specific duties:

  - Publish information to demonstrate how they are complying with the equality duty

  - Prepare and publish one or more specific and measurable equality objective.

Schools are required to update every year since 6th April 2012. The duty is non-delegable (i.e. the school must comply with the duty itself rather than giving responsibility for the duty to someone else).

What this means is that schools must:[407]

- Consider, when making a decision or taking an action, whether it may have implications for people with particular protected characteristics

- Consider equality implications before and at the time that it develops policy and takes decisions, and keep them under review

- Consciously consider each aspect of the duty separately

- Assess the risk and extent of any adverse impact that might result from a policy or decision, and the ways in which the risk might be eliminated, before adopting a proposed policy or decision

---

407 *Public Sector Equality Duty Guidance for Schools in England*, EHRC, page 7–8

- Integrate the PSED into the way it carries out its functions, and not just as a tick-box exercise

- Record the steps that the school has taken to meet the duty

The PSED does not – as of 1st October 2024 – give rise to a specific claim under the Equality Act (see R (TZA) v A Secondary School [2023] EWHC 1722 (Admin)).

This area of law is in flux with an appeal of TZA underway. If a parent wanted to allege that a school had failed to comply with the PSED, the most appropriate claim would be a claim for judicial review. Such a claim would be highly unlikely to affect or change the outcome of an individual discriminatory decision to exclude a specific pupil. But the duty, if a school carries it out rigorously, does make it more likely that a school will identify, for example, a danger of a particular policy making it more likely that pupils with a particular protected characteristic may be excluded or at increased risk of exclusion. And it is important for parents and schools to be aware that schools are under a specific duty to consider the impact upon equality of their policies, procedures and functions.

Finally, it is worth noting that the First-tier Tribunal has neither any jurisdiction to entertain a claim under section 149, nor will it be relevant or useful, in a claim for discrimination under sections 15 and 85(2) of the Equality Act, for the First-tier Tribunal to consider whether the PSED has been complied with.[408]

[408] *GP v The Lime Trust and EHRC* [2023] UKUT 77 (AAC)

Further reading

In addition to the other sources of information cited elsewhere in this book, the following are required reading for any parent or pupil contemplating a discrimination claim:

- *The SEND Code of Practice*, DfE statutory guidance, January 2015. Statutory guidance on Part 3 of the Children and Families Act 2014 and associated regulations. Local authorities, governing boards of all schools (**including** independent schools) and the First-tier Tribunal **must** have regard to this guidance whenever they are making decisions in relation to duties, policies and procedures under Part 3 of the CFA 2014. Relevant to any pupil who needs or is getting additional help at school due to a learning difficulty and/or disability.

- *Technical Guidance for Schools in England*, Equality and Human Rights Commission, July 2024. Highly readable and accessible guidance for parents, local authorities, governing bodies, and head teachers on the application of the Act in the schools context. This is not statutory guidance, but it is nonetheless highly persuasive as to the right approach to discrimination, and can be used as evidence in legal proceedings. It is being updated regularly and will be updated again in 2025.

APPENDIX

ORGANISATIONS PROVIDING SUPPORT TO PARENTS OF EXCLUDED SCHOOL PUPILS

- IPSEA – https://www.ipsea.org.uk
- Special Needs Jungle – http://www.specialneedsjungle.com
- Just For Kids Law – http://www.justforkidslaw.org
- The School Exclusion Project – https://schoolexclusionproject.com
- Ambitious About Autism – http://www.ambitiousaboutautism.org.uk/support/meeting_educational/school_exclusions/help.cfm
- Education Rights Alliance – http://educationalrightsalliance.blogspot.co.uk
- National Parent Partnership Network – http://www.iassnetwork.org.uk
- Coram Children Legal Centre – http://www.childrenslegalcentre.com
- Communities Empowerment Network – http://www.cenlive.org

- Children's Commissioner – http://www.childrenscommissioner.gov.uk
- UCL Access to Justice – http://www.ucl.ac.uk/laws/accesstojustice
- ACE Education – http://www.ace-ed.org.uk
- Behaviour Teach – http://behaviourteach.blogspot.co.uk

MORE BOOKS BY LAW BRIEF PUBLISHING

A selection of our other titles available now:-

'A Practical Guide to Probation Breaches and Other Applications' by Mark Thomas
'A Practical Guide to Remarriage and Divorce' by Cordelia Williams & Claire Howard
'A Practical Guide to Privacy, Transparency, Reporting Restrictions and Closed Proceedings in the Court of Protection' by Laura Mannering
'Beaumont on Barristers – A Guide to Defending Disciplinary Proceedings (Second Edition)' by Marc Beaumont
'A Practical Guide to Payments for Environmental Services' by Ben Sharples
'A Practical Guide to the Law of Pregnancy and Maternity at Work' by Rebecca Thomas
'A Practical Guide to Redundancy – Second Edition' by Philip Hyland & Collette Moore
'A Practical Guide to International Issues for Scottish Family Lawyers' by Susie Mountain, Donna McKay, Ken MacDonald
'A Practical Guide to the Law on Deprivation of Liberty' by Ben Troke
'A Practical Guide to Rights over Airspace and Subsoil – Second Edition' by Daniel Gatty
'A Practical Guide to the Law in Relation to Inquests' by Ramya Nagesh
'A Practical Guide to the Construction and Rectification of Wills and Trust Instruments (Second Edition)' by Edward Hewitt
'A Practical Guide to Data Protection in Social Housing' by Clare Paterson
'A Practical Guide to Spousal Maintenance – Second Edition' by Liz Cowell
'A Practical Guide to International Parental Child Abduction Law (England and Wales)' by Dr Onyója Momoh
'A Practical Guide to Deprivation of British Citizenship' by Sean Ell
'A Practical Guide to Commercial Property Service Charges' by Rachel Garton
'A Practical Guide to Clinical Negligence – Third Edition' by Geoffrey Simpson-Scott (Geoff)
'A Practical Guide to the Rights of Grandparents in Children Proceedings – Second Edition' by Stuart Barlow

‘The Electronic Communications Code: A Practical Guide – Second Edition’ by Kerry Bretherton KC, James Castle, Mark Loveday

‘A Practical Guide to the Independent School Standards – September 2023 Edition’ by Sarah McKimm

'A Practical Guide to Estate Administration and Crypto Assets' by Richard Marshall

‘A Practical Guide to Parental Alienation in Private and Public Law Children Cases’ by Sam King QC & Frankie Shama

‘Contested Heritage – Removing Art from Land and Historic Buildings’ by Richard Harwood QC, Catherine Dobson, David Sawtell

‘The Limits of Separate Legal Personality: When Those Running a Company Can Be Held Personally Liable for Losses Caused to Third Parties Outside of the Company’ by Dr Mike Wilkinson

‘A Practical Guide to Transgender Law’ by Robin Moira White & Nicola Newbegin

‘A Practical Guide to ‘Stranded Spouses’ in Family Law’ by Mani Singh Basi

‘A Practical Guide to Residential Freehold Conveyancing’ by Lorraine Richardson

‘A Practical Guide to Pensions on Divorce for Lawyers’ by Bryan Scant

‘A Practical Guide to Challenging Sham Marriage Allegations in Immigration Law’ by Priya Solanki

‘A Practical Guide to Digital Communications Evidence in Criminal Law’ by Sam Willis

‘A Practical Guide to Legal Rights in Scotland’ by Sarah-Jane Macdonald

‘A Practical Guide to New Build Conveyancing’ by Paul Sams & Rebecca East

‘A Practical Guide to Inherited Wealth on Divorce’ by Hayley Trim

‘A Practical Guide to Practice Direction 12J and Domestic Abuse in Private Law Children Proceedings’ by Rebecca Cross & Malvika Jaganmohan

‘A Practical Guide to Confiscation and Restraint’ by Narita Bahra QC, John Carl Townsend, David Winch

‘A Practical Guide to the Law of Forests in Scotland’ by Philip Buchan

‘A Practical Guide to Health and Medical Cases in Immigration Law’ by Rebecca Chapman & Miranda Butler

‘A Practical Guide to Bad Character Evidence for Criminal Practitioners by Aparna Rao

‘A Practical Guide to Extradition Law post-Brexit’ by Myles Grandison et al

‘A Practical Guide to Hoarding and Mental Health for Housing Lawyers’ by Rachel Coyle

‘Stephens on Contractual Indemnities’ by Richard Stephens

‘A Practical Guide to the EU Succession Regulation’ by Richard Frimston

‘A Practical Guide to Solicitor and Client Costs – Second Edition’ by Robin Dunne

‘Constructive Dismissal – Practice Pointers and Principles’ by Benjimin Burgher

‘A Practical Guide to Religion and Belief Discrimination Claims in the Workplace’ by Kashif Ali

‘A Practical Guide to the Law of Medical Treatment Decisions’ by Ben Troke

‘Fundamental Dishonesty and QOCS in Personal Injury Proceedings: Law and Practice’ by Jake Rowley

‘A Practical Guide to the Law in Relation to School Exclusions’ by Charlotte Hadfield & Alice de Coverley

‘A Practical Guide to Divorce for the Silver Separators’ by Karin Walker

‘The Right to be Forgotten – The Law and Practical Issues’ by Melissa Stock

‘A Practical Guide to Planning Law and Rights of Way in National Parks, the Broads and AONBs’ by James Maurici QC, James Neill et al

‘A Practical Guide to Election Law’ by Tom Tabori

‘A Practical Guide to the Law in Relation to Surrogacy’ by Andrew Powell

‘A Practical Guide to Claims Arising from Fatal Accidents – Second Edition’ by James Patience

‘A Practical Guide to Asbestos Claims’ by Jonathan Owen & Gareth McAloon

‘A Practical Guide to Stamp Duty Land Tax in England and Northern Ireland’ by Suzanne O’Hara

‘A Practical Guide to the Law of Farming Partnerships’ by Philip Whitcomb

‘A Practical Guide to the Law of Unlawful Eviction and Harassment – Second Edition’ by Stephanie Lovegrove

‘A Practical Guide to Costs in Personal Injury Claims – Second Edition’ by Matthew Hoe

‘A Practical Guide to the General Data Protection Regulation (GDPR) – Second Edition’ by Keith Markham

‘A Practical Guide to Working with Litigants in Person and McKenzie Friends in Family Cases’ by Stuart Barlow

‘Protecting Unregistered Brands: A Practical Guide to the Law of Passing Off’ by Lorna Brazell

‘A Practical Guide to Secondary Liability and Joint Enterprise Post-Jogee’ by Joanne Cecil & James Mehigan

'A Practical Guide to the Pre-Action RTA Claims Protocol for Personal Injury Lawyers' by Antonia Ford

'A Practical Guide to Neighbour Disputes and the Law' by Alexander Walsh

'A Practical Guide to Coercive Control for Legal Practitioners and Victims' by Rachel Horman

'A Practical Guide to the Law of Driverless Cars – Second Edition'

by Alex Glassbrook, Emma Northey & Scarlett Milligan

'A Practical Guide to TOLATA Claims' by Greg Williams

'A Practical Guide to Elderly Law – Second Edition' by Justin Patten

'A Practical Guide to Responding to Housing Disrepair and Unfitness Claims' by Iain Wightwick

'A Practical Guide to the Law of Bullying and Harassment in the Workplace' by Philip Hyland

'How to Be a Freelance Solicitor: A Practical Guide to the SRA-Regulated Freelance Solicitor Model' by Paul Bennett

'A Practical Guide to Prison Injury Claims' by Malcolm Johnson

'A Practical Guide to Advising Clients at the Police Station' by Colin Stephen McKeown-Beaumont

'A Practical Guide to Antisocial Behaviour Injunctions – Second Edition' by Iain Wightwick

'Practical Mediation: A Guide for Mediators, Advocates, Advisers, Lawyers, and Students in Civil, Commercial, Business, Property, Workplace, and Employment Cases' by Jonathan Dingle with John Sephton

'The Mini-Pupillage Workbook' by David Boyle

'A Practical Guide to Crofting Law' by Brian Inkster

'A Practical Guide to the Law of Domain Names and Cybersquatting' by Andrew Clemson

'A Practical Guide to the Law of Gender Pay Gap Reporting' by Harini Iyengar

'NHS Whistleblowing and the Law' by Joseph England

'Employment Law and the Gig Economy' by Nigel Mackay & Annie Powell

'A Practical Guide to Noise Induced Hearing Loss (NIHL) Claims' by Andrew Mckie, Ian Skeate, Gareth McAloon

'An Introduction to Beauty Negligence Claims – A Practical Guide for the Personal Injury Practitioner' by Greg Almond

'Intercompany Agreements for Transfer Pricing Compliance' by Paul Sutton

'Zen and the Art of Mediation' by Martin Plowman

'A Practical Guide to Adoption for Family Lawyers' by Graham Pegg

www.ingramcontent.com/pod-product-compliance
Lightning Source LLC
LaVergne TN
LVHW052300200926
848481LV00002B/420
9781916698628